HIDDEN
HERTFORDSHIRE

HIDDEN

HERTFORDSHIRE

Jeffery W Whitelaw

With illustrations by Pip Challenger
from photographs by the author

COUNTRYSIDE BOOKS
NEWBURY, BERKSHIRE

First Published 1988
© Jeffery W Whitelaw 1988

COUNTRYSIDE BOOKS
3 Catherine Road
Newbury, Berkshire

ISBN 1 85306 025 9

Cover photograph of the Old Church, Ayot St Lawrence
taken by the author

Produced through MRM Associates, Reading
Typeset by Acorn Bookwork, Salisbury
Printed in England by J. W. Arrowsmith Ltd, Bristol

Bibliography and Further Reading

Pevsner's *Buildings of England – Hertfordshire* always accompanied us on our field trips but I would like to list the books which were consulted during the time I was working on my book.

Royal Commission on Historical Monuments – An Inventory of the Historical Monuments in Hertfordshire H.M. Stationery Office 1910

Sir Nikolaus Pevsner and Bridget Cherry *The Buildings of England – Hertfordshire* 2nd Ed. Penguin 1977

Arthur Mee *The Kings England – Hertfordshire* Hodder and Stoughton. 1939

R. M. Healey *Shell Guide to Hertfordshire* Faber 1982

H. M. Alderman *A Pilgrimage in Hertfordshire* Trefoil 1931

Gover, Mawer and Stenton *The Place-Names of Hertfordshire* C.U.P. 1938

Sir William Beach Thomas *Hertfordshire* Robt. Hale 1950

Herts Federation of Women's Institutes *The Hertfordshire Village Book* Countryside Books, 1986

Herbert W. Tompkins *Little Guide to Hertfordshire* 1st ed. Methuen 1903

W. Branch Johnson *Little Guide to Hertfordshire* 2nd Ed. Methuen 1957

W. Branch Johnson *Industrial Archaeology of Hertfordshire* David and Charles 1970

Herts County Council *Hertfordshire – A County Guide* British Publishing Company Ltd. 1986

Back issues of the county magazine *Hertfordshire Countryside*

Introduction

When I was invited to write a book entitled *Hidden Hertford-shire*, I thought that here was something 'right up my street'. I have been a resident of Harpenden for 34 years – almost half a lifetime – and during those years I have amassed some 4000 photographs of the county, been a regular contributor to the county magazine *Hertfordshire Countryside* for all of that time and a writer on local architecture etc more recently for one of the St Albans free papers.

The use of the word 'hidden' was not to imply that the book would reveal subjects, places or things which were concealed – but a word to be used to draw attention to subjects which were not the usual guidebook material, or places and things normally overlooked. The book was to be part of a series, each one entitled *Hidden Surrey*, *Hidden Sussex* or wherever, and, as a collector of 'curiosities' or 'oddities' around the county for many years, I thought that it would be 'a piece of cake'!

How wrong I was and as I write this Introduction at the end of six months of concentrated research and effort, I realise with humility just how little I knew then of this small but beautiful county.

Hertfordshire, at the beginning of the century, was the venue for the first purpose-built Garden City at Letchworth and again, in the late 1940s Stevenage was the first of the New Towns planned after the Second World War, so the county's pioneering spirit was carried forward. However, despite the four New Towns in the county, there are still quite large areas, particularly in the much more open northern parts, which are as seemingly remote, and largely unspoilt, as anywhere in the whole country.

It was a growing awareness of these more remote areas that caused me to realise just how small was my knowledge and many hours have been spent on field trips, seeing new places, checking on facts and attempting to visit churches, with my wife busy making notes while I sought out anything which we had listed to see before the visit.

On the subject of the county's churches, I would mention here that a typical church of Hertfordshire has an embattled parapet to the tower with what is known as a 'spike' (an alternative name being the 'snuffer') on top and there are many examples of what Sir Nikolaus Pevsner calls 'extremely thin recessed spires' in various shapes and sizes. Attention is drawn, accordingly, to those churches which do not conform to the usual pattern, eg Holy Cross at Sarratt and St Thomas the Martyr at Northaw. Attention is also drawn to 'pudding-stone' in several villages, which has been used in the structure of churches or just left lying about in great lumps as at Standon. The late Alec Clifton-Taylor, in an appendix to Pevsner's *Buildings of Hertfordshire* (Penguin) wrote: 'The only other stone native to Hertfordshire is the humble puddingstone – it is a material which nobody would think of using for building unless he had nothing better; but in Hertfordshire this was sometimes the case. So sections of puddingstone wall can be seen at a number of churches, yet at none does it offer any aesthetic enjoyment'.

I must make two comments with regards to churches. First, in common with the practice of other works in this series, I have not referred to any articles of portable value in the interiors of churches for very obvious reasons and, secondly, be cautious in your viewing of lychgates. In comparison with the total number of churches, there are only about three dozen: some of these are very old but several are modern, acting merely to serve as an entrance to the churchyard with no historical or religious significance.

Reference is made in a number of the entries to the restoration work undertaken by Sir George Gilbert Scott (1811–1878), best known for the Albert Memorial and St Pancras Station, or more correctly, The Midland Grand Hotel at St Pancras. Let it not be forgotten, however, that the very first church of which he was the architect was built at Flaunden in 1838. He also built Holy Trinity at Frogmore on Watling Street, St John's at Bourne End and the little chapel at Childwick Green.

A number of authors like Pevsner or Arthur Mee crop up

all the way through this book and I make no apology for this. The late Sir Nikolaus Pevsner's *Buildings of England* series published by Penguin Books, a marvellous collection of books without parallel covering every county, has been my 'bible' and architectural inspiration ever since the books started to be published – with the 1st edition of *Hertfordshire* being one of the earliest. Likewise, Arthur Mee's book, written before the Second World War, has been helpful, even if a little inaccurate, but my constant reference to the *Little Guide* of 1903 has been a deliberate attempt to highlight contrasts of today with a period which sometimes seems 850 years ago rather than only 85!

Above all, I must pay tribute to the late and sadly-missed county historian W. Branch Johnson. He was honoured by both The Royal Historical Society and The Society of Anti-quaries for all the work he did for and the books he had written about the county over many years. His books included the virtual re-writing of the Herbert W. Tompkins' *Little Guide* (mentioned above) which was published in 1953 but one of his last works was a little edited version of *The Carrington Diary* for which I took photographs for him of original diary pages preserved in the County Records Office in Hertford. Perhaps he felt that his task was all but done because, in lieu of cash, he gave me his own annotated list edition of *The Royal Commission on Historical Monuments – An Inventory of the Historical Monuments in Hertfordshire* – a reward which no money could equal. I shall always be grateful to him for this and so, along with the *Buildings of Hertfordshire* (Pevsner), this book, published in 1910 and the very first of the Royal Commission's volumes (and the end is still not in sight!) has a mention here and there in the entries.

I think that I must mention one more book in connection with the plaque on the church of St Paul's Walden because some royalists may take exception to my denial of its contents. I would refer the doubters to *The Queen Mother* by Anthony Holden, published by Shere Books Ltd in 1985 as a birthday tribute to Her Majesty The Queen Mother. Anthony Holden is a well-known writer on the Royal Family and all his books are officially authorised – so my defence rests!

One or two explanatory comments are called for because, obviously, not every one who uses this book will be knowledgeable in church architecture etc. An 'apse' is a vaulted semi-circular or polygonal end of a chancel or chapel. A 'corbel' is a block of stone supporting some feature on its horizontal top surface. A 'misericord' is a small hinged seat with brackets placed on the underside, usually carved with figures which, when turned up, give the occupant support during long periods of standing – especially for the aged. A 'poppyhead' is a carved ornament of leaves or flowers used to decorate tops of bench or stall ends – somewhat resembling a fleur-de-lys. The 'rood' is a cross or crucifix, with the 'rood screen' the screen below the rood – usually between the chancel and the nave. One other point – where 'O.S.' is used this refers to the Ordnance Survey maps available in any good bookshop.

And so to a few acknowledgements and apologies. Many guides and church guides were used and consulted for greater accuracy and I am grateful to the writers of these aids. To any author who may consider that I have used his words without acknowledgement – research often results in only one suitable comment on the subject involved – I offer my humble apologies.

Finally, I must thank my wife who not only helped with all the research on the field work and had to put up with all my excuses about 'having to get on with my book' for six months when trying to get me to do some domestic chore, but did most of the typing as well in order to meet the publisher's deadline!

Jeffery W Whitelaw

The four-sided clock of the 17th century barn at Pimlico

Abbots Langley

In St Lawrence's church a stone tablet, erected by the Hertfordshire Historical Society in 1924, is inscribed thus: 'At Bedmond, in this parish, about the date of this present church, was born Nicholas Breakspear, Pope Adrian IV (1154–1159), the only English Pope'.

Nicholas Breakspear was born circa 1100 in Bedmond, the son of Robert Breakspear who became a monk in the Abbey of St Albans and who, apparently, left the boy to his own devices. When Nicholas also attempted to enter the Community he was rejected by the Abbot on account of his ignorance and his youth. Bitterly disappointed but spurred on by his ardour for study, he begged his way to France and, after entering the Abbey of St Rufus near Avignon in a menial capacity, eventually became its Abbot! His zeal brought him the notice of Pope Eugenius III, who made him a Cardinal and sent him to convert the heathen in Norway and Sweden.

The day after Pope Anastasius' death in 1154, Nicholas Breakspear, the English Cardinal, was elected 'with unanimous voice' to be his successor and he became Pope Adrian IV, the only English Pope. Sadly, although he had a momentous reign, he died after only five years in 1159.

There is much speculation as to Breakspear's birthplace in the hamlet of Bedmond, now separated from Abbots Langley by the M25 motorway, although Breakspear Farm (a 17th century building) was probably built on the site of the original birthplace.

No doubt about the Roman Catholic Breakspear College, formerly Langley House, and the 1963 St. Saviour's Roman Catholic church with its modernistic sculpture facing The Crescent – they will help to perpetuate the memory of the only Englishman to become Pope.

Between this little complex and the valley of the M25, do not miss the former Ovaltine Dairy Farm – this has been converted into a prestigious range of housing called

11

Antoinette Court. Antoinette Court – surely a curious name in Hertfordshire? The developers claim that the name was chosen because 'this Dairy was originally erected to the same design as that built for Marie Antoinette in Versailles'.

Much of Abbots Langley is taken up with housing estates, hospitals and Leavesden airport, so, with a passing mention of the modern library close by, and the Georgian rectory behind, it is into St. Lawrence's church through the lychgate that you must go for the rest of your stay in Abbots Langley.

The dates on the tablet are misleading – the church was dedicated in 1154 the year that Nicholas Breakspear became Pope and *not* when he was born. Be that as it may, the church celebrated its 800th anniversary in 1954, and despite a fire in 1969, much of the Norman structure remains. The massive west tower, formerly embattled and plus a spike, now has neither, but it dates right back to 1200. There is a font of circa 1400 and nearby a Table of Commandments (note the omission of 'the maidservant' from the 10th commandment), but the south chapel with its wall painting and the 1640 Purbeck marble memorial of Anne Coombe are real treasures.

Albury

➤ Do not confuse this village – which lies a mile or so off the A120, the old Roman Stane Street between Puckeridge and Little Hadham – with the village spelt with a 'd' in the name (see below) in the Chilterns. This village is a straggly one, and appears to be split into three parts.

After leaving the A120 and making for the centre of the village, note first the house at Albury End with the huge oriel window. Built only in the late 1950s, it jars far less than some other modern houses erected with no thought for conservation or their surroundings.

Before you reach the school and St Mary's church, and on the same side of the road there is an attractive house called The Labour in Vain – this was formerly an inn which had a sign depicting a white woman scrubbing a black baby. St. Mary's chancel dates back to the 13th century although the tall tower, complete with Hertfordshire spike, was built in 1450. There are some old brasses on the floor and the south wall, but they are not as old as the defaced effigies of a knight and his lady of circa 1400 showing costume and armour of the period on a tomb chest by the north wall. A massive oak chest stands by this tomb, and outside note the little statuette in a niche on the south wall. Before leaving this part of the village do not miss the village pond opposite and the 16th century cottage right next to the church, renovated now but still with its leaning walls.

The road to Furneaux Pelham leads through the third part of the village, where stands the weather-boarded Catherine Wheel and its unusual sign but beware! It keeps somewhat haphazard opening hours!

Aldbury

Aldbury, in living memory and earlier, can hardly be classed as being 'hidden'. Visitors have been coming here since late Victorian times and its proximity to Ashridge and the Bridgewater Monument virtually guarantees a lack of privacy.

The stocks and whipping post by the pond backed by the half timbered Yeoman's House, apparently unchanged over many centuries, present a picture of the archetypal English Village, perhaps even more so than Westmill on the other side of the county.

The village contains a number of attractive 16th and 17th century cottages, some being half timbered and some, including the old almshouses, are pargetted. In the garden of the Chantry cottages and facing the stocks is a curious brick building which was at one time a communal well house, wash-house cum bake-house – it is unique in the county. Another treasure, a sundial on a 17th century post which used to stand in the churchyard, you will *not* be able to find

The stocks and whipping post at Aldbury

because the whole thing was stolen one night in the 1980s. If caught, the stocks and whipping post could perhaps be brought back into use for the miscreant – they were last used in the middle of the 19th century!

The church itself has a number of interesting features, particularly a stone screen separating the Pendley Chapel off from the rest of the church. In the chapel the tomb of Sir Robert Whittingham, who died in 1452 and whose feet rest on what has become known as 'The Wild Man' who clutches a thick staff, is a particularly fine example of 15th century work.

Also in the church are monuments to the Duncombe family who owned, for 500 years, the house and estate known as 'Stocks'. In 1891 it passed by inheritance to Lord Grey of Falloden. He, in turn, sold it to T. Humphrey Ward, the husband of Mrs. Humphrey Ward (a grand-daughter of the famous Dr Arnold of Rugby) who was a popular novelist in the early years of the century, although more or less forgotten now. She died in 1920, and is buried in the church-yard but it must not be forgotten that she took a deep interest in social work and that she was one of the first women magistrates.

There are neither battlements nor spike on the tower but it does date back to the 14th century, and the two-storeyed porch is probably of the same period. Both tower and porch were restored in 1905 by the children of Fanny Wood in her memory – she was the widow of a one-time rector here. The lychgate is modern.

Aldenham

The parish of Aldenham, boxed in on all sides – by the M25 to the north, by the M1 to the west and by the Bedpan Line, together with old Watling Street to the east – and with the centre of London only 14 miles away, still manages, apparently, to preserve an appearance of rural charm. In actual fact, the parish itself consists of the two little villages of Aldenham and Letchmore Heath and a number of large houses of which many have been turned into schools or out-of-town offices for organisations, and the rural charm is systematically broken by planes using Elstree aerodrome or stacking overhead waiting to land at Heathrow!

Aldenham House is the oldest of these large houses, and it now houses the Haberdashers' Aske's Boys School, but the lands, originally purchased by the 1st Lord Aldenham when the house belonged to him, have now become the Aldenham Country Park complete with a lake – formerly a reservoir.

Sandwiched between the aerodrome and the top end of the Hilfield Park or New Reservoir, just west of the Country Park, is Hilfield Castle, a Gothic fantasy complete with portcullis, built circa 1805 by Sir Jeffry Wyatville, one of the architect family very much involved with Ashridge over several generations. Down a drive leading straight out of Aldenham village itself is Wall Hall, another Gothic creation – this time complete with some artificial ruins – which is now part of Hatfield Polytechnic.

Aldenham Public School, as far as the postman is concerned, is situated in Letchmore Heath, and so is the big house now called 'Bhaktivedanta Manor' which is owned by the Krishna Consciousness Sect. The school was founded in 1599 by a London brewer, one Richard Platt, and was greatly enlarged in 1825 to become what it is today – a flourishing public school. One of Aldenham's Old Boys was Sir Alfred Gilbert who is best known for his figure of Eros in the centre of Piccadilly Circus.

The little village of Letchmore Heath itself is an oasis of 16th century cottages, a 16th century inn The Three Horseshoes by the village green and the village pond – truly amazing when you think of the closeness to London and the fact that most of the inhabitants today are commuters.

Although the Social Club has 16th century timberwork hidden behind the 19th century front, and the former 18th century vicarage adjoining the churchyard is of interest, Aldenham village is not much more than a hamlet so finally it is the impressive church of St. John the Baptist which dominates the area because of its tall tower – made even higher by its stair turret and spike. Inside are many treasures including a 13th century font of Purbeck marble, a huge chest dated of the 14th century, many brasses and an unusual monument comprising identical tomb chests to two ladies of the Crowmer family, again of the 14th century.

Anstey

◣ Domesday Book showed that Anestige was already a village when Count Eustace of Boulogne, who fought with the Conqueror at The Battle of Hastings, came into possession of the manor. It is probable that he built the castle which was itself destroyed in Henry III's reign. Although there is no sign of masonry, the great motte and bailey remain, surrounded by a moat, situated just behind the church. Its very survival after so many centuries helped to save a large part of the village from destruction when, in October 1944, an American Flying Fortress bomber failed to become properly airborne after taking off from nearby Nuthampstead, and burst into flames after hitting the castle mound. The crew died immediately but the force of the impact had pitched the bombs into the soft mud of the moat – had they exploded then nearby St. George's church would have been flattened along with Anstey Hall.

A local legend attached to the castle concerns a blind fiddler and his dog who set out one day to test the truth of a local belief about a passage connecting a chalk pit with the castle dungeons: the local myth was that anyone venturing into it would never come out alive. It is said that Blind George the Fiddler, all the while playing his fiddle, disappeared into the passage but his fiddle playing grew fainter and fainter until, after a loud shriek, it was heard no more. The dog reappeared, terrified and without a hair on its body, and fled and, like foolhardy Blind George, was never seen again! It all happened – if it happened at all – well over 200 years ago but do not scoff at the local legend when in Anstey!

St. George's church, from some angles, looks like a castle itself and some authorities consider Count Eustace may have had a hand in its construction. Certainly parts of it are very early Norman and full details can be found in the informative pamphlet on sale inside.

Misericords are usually only found in the choir stalls of great cathedrals but there are seven here – a most unusual treasure in a village church. Note also the crude Norman font with four mermen holding their split tails with both their hands: this design is another rarity with the only other one in England being in St. Peter's church, Cambridge.

Outside, return to the village via the 15th century lychgate and on departure you will see that one-third of it has been converted into a lock-up. This was bricked up in 1831 and was still in use as late as 1914.

In the village there are a number of architecturally interesting houses and cottages with quite a few dating back to the 17th and even 16th century but do not miss another curiosity on the wall of Rose Cottage! Before the Second World War every village had a round yellow AA sign showing the village name, and various distances from it. Removed during the war, about a dozen have reappeared and this is the only one in Hertfordshire.

At the road junction for Nuthampstead an old well has been preserved – the complicated wheel system under its gabled roof will keep you guessing as to how it worked, but you will keep dry!

Ardeley

➤ Ardeley, the centre point of several small hamlets, has a pre-Domesday Book history but a formal village green of only 1917. At the height of the First World War, the lord of the manor, John Howard Carter, who owned the land, and the vicar, Dr. Eek, had a vision of better times, and the result was the horseshoe of thatched cottages around the green with a functioning well in the middle. At one side is the unusual-looking village hall with its wooden pillars which was built after the war was over.

Just across the road from the green is the village war memorial and a pond standing immediately in front of St. Lawrence's church. It has an embattled tower with a fine spike but the chief delight is the 15th century roof which is supported by 12 carved wooden angels all playing musical instruments. There are some 15th century benches with poppyhead ends and the font is another octagonal one, probably 15th century also.

The manor itself, Ardeley Bury, although not open to the public, is down a long drive to the west of the church and is basically Tudor. It was here that Sir Henry Chauncy, the author of The Historical Antiquities of Hertfordshire, was born in 1632. He was knighted in 1681 and was the first Recorder of Hertford, and was also involved in condemning Jane Wenham as a witch (see Walkern). The Bury was 'gothicized' with turrets and battlements in 1820 with the original moat becoming a lake.

Arkley

➤ Technically in Greater London since the boundary revisions of 1964, no self-respecting writer would dream – or even dare – of omitting Arkley from a description of the county especially as the village, like its big brother Barnet, retains 'Hertfordshire' in any address label.

Purely as a matter of interest, an enclosed monastery was built here in Galley Lane as recently as 1968 – a move from Notting Hill – but the visual elements are The Gate public house and a restored tower mill in the garden opposite at a spot known as Barnet Gate. Originally built in 1806, great efforts have been made to preserve this now listed building but, being so exposed, there is little protection from hurricanes such as the one experienced in October 1987!

Ashwell

➤ Ashwell is, without doubt, the most interesting village in the whole county with something to hold your attention at every turn and the whole place is dominated from any viewpoint in the village, and from all around, by the magnificent tower, octagonal lantern and spike totalling 176 feet of St. Mary's church.

In complete contrast, just off the road leading into the High Street, is what is known as Ashwell Springs. This is where the river Rhee bubbles up through the chalk and the little plaque nearby proclaims that this is the source of the river Cam.

At the time of Domesday Book, Escewelle was already established because of its proximity to the Icknield Way and, in fact, there is evidence that the place grew out of the Iron Age fort of Arbury Banks to the south-west. The length of its history, and the fact that there is no major highway bearing heavy loads have combined to preserve a great range of buildings of many centuries.

In the High Street is the Guildhall of St. John the Baptist of circa 1476 next door to the Guildhouse with its fine decorative pargetting and the figure of a dolphin, even a date of 1681, and opposite the beautifully restored Foresters Cottages – as fine a group as may be found anywhere, even in East Anglia!

Elsewhere the 500 year old Town House in Swan Street, saved from demolition by the efforts of caring village people in the 1920s, is now a museum, where bygones and pamphlets giving information on Ashwell may be found. A lock-up in Hodwell, the Merchant Taylor's school (now a library) in Mill Street, the old mill itself (now a private house but retaining its gigantic water-wheel) and a thatched wall in Gardiners Lane are but a few more of the treasures to be found in Ashwell.

So to another look at St. Mary's church. Its very size reflects Ashwell's past prosperity as a one-time market town, but now it is the exterior which is a reminder of past glory and, as Pevsner puts it, the interior is 'decidedly puritanical, especially as the church has surprisingly little of furnishings'. The pulpit is dated 1627 and there is a bench end of the 15th century on which is carved a fish but of peculiar interest is the drawing of Old St. Paul's of circa 1350 on the wall of the tower together with some Latin doggerel recalling the Black Death which translated reads as: '1350 Miserable, wild and distracted, the dregs of the people alone survive to witness . . . etc'.

Aspenden

➤ Whether you approach this architecturally interesting village from Westmill or under the bypass from Buntingford, the long winding street ends abruptly at the church of St. Mary – beyond that is only a gate leading to the grey mansion of the Tudor Stud, the original Aspenden Hall.

A variety of cottages, dating from several centuries, crowd in on the single street, a number with pargetting – even an overhang here and there – but note The Bell House, and Aspenden Lodge with its columns on either side of the porch.

Aspenden Hall, between 1813 and 1825, was run as a school by the Revd Matthew Morris Preston, and it was here that young Thomas Babbington Macaulay, later to become Lord Macaulay, the historian, came in 1814 and stayed until 1816. Bishop Seth Ward, who was born in the village in 1618, became Bishop of Salisbury, Chancellor of The Order of the Garter and the second President of The Royal Society (see Buntingford).

The nave and chancel of the church are late 11th century but the south chancel chapel was built in the 15th century and remodelled in 1622. The south porch was built in 1525 by the widow of Sir Robert Clifford who died in 1508, and lies beneath a tomb chest in the south chapel. The two-light window spaces in the south porch are fitted with stained glass of the four evangelists (two on each side) by Morris & Co – perhaps the last Pre-Raphaelite glass.

Aston

➤ Aston and Aston End, on the eastern fringe of ever-growing Stevenage, may escape being over-run but the planners may think otherwise. Let us hope so because the village, like the 13th century church, has a long history with Estone being an entry in Domesday Book.

Modern in-filling has taken place but both in Aston and Aston End a number of listed buildings have been carefully restored. A mile to the south stands Astonbury, a fine example of an Elizabethan house with its ornate original chimneys to be seen but not visited.

While it was being built circa 1540 John Kent was beginning his long stewardship in the household of not only

Edward VI but also Queen Mary and Queen Elizabeth I. You will find a brass of 1592 to this good and faithful servant plus his wife on the floor of the nave of St. Mary's. Nothing special otherwise but the pulpit is circa 1630 and there is a screen of circa 1500.

Ayot St. Lawrence

This tiny hamlet, one of the prettiest in the county, would have remained fairly isolated and perhaps largely ignored, as far as anywhere can be today, except for one vital factor. George Bernard Shaw, the Irish dramatist, bought the New Rectory in 1906 and lived there until his death, at the age of 94, in 1950. Some of his famous plays, like *Arms and The Man*, *Major Barbara* and *Man and Superman* were written before coming to Ayot, but arguably the equally famous – and probably best known – like *Pygmalion* and *Saint Joan*, not forgetting *The Apple Cart*, were all written at the New Rectory.

Now, renamed Shaw's Corner before his death when the building was given to the National Trust in 1944 after the death of his wife in 1943, his home is a place of pilgrimage. The downstairs rooms are kept as they were in his lifetime and the little hut in the garden in which he did his writing is just as he left it. They even sell teas here when you visit in the summer in this, the only National Trust building open to the public in the county.

Attractive half-timbered cottages, and the Brocket Arms inn make up a large part of the south side of the tiny village street but opposite is the ruined 12th century church of St. Lawrence. Now called the 'old' church but neither abandoned nor made redundant like Caldecote or Layston, it was the victim of the then lord of the manor, Sir Lionel Lyde. In 1778 he built what is now called the 'new' St. Lawrence: the architect was Nicholas Revett who also designed St. Pancras' church in London and who specialised in the classical touch – in short, he virtually designed a Greek Temple! The church was partly to boost Sir Lionel's new-found status and, apparently to serve as an eye-catcher from the manor. Some of the old church had been demolished to help provide materials for the new but the Bishop of Lincoln prevented further destruction and so the building remains as a picturesque ruin – an eye-catcher indeed but too dangerous to visit! Note the wrought iron gate.

Incidentally, the new church has the altar at the west end, the reverse of what is customary. This was done in order that the doorway, with its four-column portico and the two pavilions might be placed at the end facing Ayot House. Concerts and an Art Exhibition are held in the church each mid-summer.

Ayot St. Peter

➤ Whether approached by narrow lanes from its more famous neighbour, or from the Old North Road (now the B197), Ayot St. Peter deserves a place here because, in its own quiet way, and undisturbed by the A1(M) which is sunk in a deep cutting, it retains the old village concept of cottages around the village green. The cottages may now all belong to commuters, the old estate labourers long gone, but the present incumbents are jealous of their attractive site and strict planning laws keep incomers on the straight and narrow. Note St. Peter's church, built in 1875 with a most untypical broach spire and its fancifully designed clock face.

Baldock

➤ Although there was a Roman settlement where Roman Icknield Way and Stane Street crossed, confirmed by considerable archaeological work in the present century, Baldock's history really starts in 1145 when it was founded by the Knights Templars – the name is derived from their word for Baghdad.

The wide High Street and the many old inns reflect its importance in coaching days as it lay on the Great North Road and a stroll round the town with a guidebook will reveal not only some unusually large Georgian mansions but also a variety of buildings from many centuries including the half-timbered 17th century Bull's Head Inn in Church Street and Wynne's Almshouses built 1623 in the High Street itself.

John Wynne built six red brick almshouses, each with a small porch, a mullioned window on the ground floor and a dormer window in the roof. The inscription over the gateway reads: 'These Alms Houses are the Gift of Mr JOHN WYNN Citizen and Mercht. of LONDON lately deceased, who hath left a yearly Stipend to every Poor of Either House to the worlds End – Sep. Anno Dom 1623'. The worthy benefactor's name over the gateway is as shown above, 'Wynn' but there is another inscription on the wall of the building spelling it as 'Wynne'.

Tesco's supermarket in the old Kaysor Bonder stocking factory – undoubtedly a fine building – may now be the most dominant place in the town but the church, standing as it does right in the centre, is still the town's greatest feature and full of architectural interest.

The early 14th century embattled tower has its 'spike' but this stands on top of a lantern so ensuring that the church, although hardly noticed when in the middle of the town, is seen from many miles all around. Actually most of the church is of the 14th century, having been almost entirely rebuilt in circa 1330 but its set of screens which stretch right across from aisle to aisle, including a more ornate rood screen are of the 15th century. There are many little architectural features here which a church guide will reveal, but before leaving the churchyard by the gate into Church Street do not miss the sad story on a graveboard–

'How soon I was cut down, when innocent at play
The wind it blew a scaffold down and took my Life away'.

Barkway

➤ Berg Cottage dated 1687 at the southern end of the single, long, High Street and one of a number of 16th or 17th century half-timbered houses in Barkway, was given to the National Trust in 1938 but is not open to the public. So what is there to see in this once important market town (a market charter was granted by Henry III but long ago discontinued) and coach stopping place, apart from the almshouses which stand opposite Berg Cottage?

Truthfully not a lot except that the village street, taken as a whole, seems to retain a dignity through surviving many centuries and, luckily, escaping being turned into a major highway. In the High Street, near the turning down to the church of St. Mary Magdalene, is one of the remaining 'Trinity Milestones' set up in 1725 by Dr. William Warren, Master of Trinity Hall, between Barkway and Cambridge. These milestones were erected by Dr. Warren in consequence of two bequests, made 150 years earlier by two Elizabethan Fellows of Trinity – Dr. Mouse and Robert Hare – towards the maintenance of highways between Cambridge and Barkway. Each milestone bears the arms of Trinity Hall and the distance from Cambridge.

The church itself has a history similar to so many. It has a 13th century chancel and was restored in Victorian times – although there are still angels, toads, rabbits and other carvings visible on the corbels supporting the 15th century roof. The tower, originally built early in the 15th century, was entirely rebuilt almost from the foundations in 1861 and, when completed, they stuck four pinnacles on the top – a most un-Hertfordshire feature!

Barley

➤ Can you believe your eyes? Hounds are chasing a fox above the road into the pub called The Fox and Hounds. Actually this inn sign with effigies of huntsmen and dogs chasing a fox along a beam slung across the road is the first thing that you see as you drop down into the village from Barkway. The name of the inn dates back to the early 18th century when a fox did, in fact, flee into a gap in the thatch to escape the hounds: this sign, however, is only to keep the old story alive because the original inn which was elsewhere in the village was burnt down in 1950, and the present inn changed its name from The Waggon and Horses! Not all the villagers agreed with the switch but it is good for tourism!

Barley, practically on the Cambridgeshire border, has a very long history and was well established by the time of Domesday Book. Most of the older cottages are, however, only of the 17th century as is the cage or lock-up on Cross-hill. The main antiquity is The Town House, formerly The Guildhall, which lies just across the road from the church – and, in its time, school and almshouses. Built early in the 16th century and beautifully restored through voluntary communal effort between 1969 and 1972, it is now once again the village hall and the centre for most of the activities in the village.

Wedding receptions are, of course, one of the activities after ceremonies in St. Margaret the Martyr opposite which, although it still retains its Norman tower, was more or less rebuilt in 1872 by the architect William Butterfield. Despite his restoration, there are a number of old artefacts including the 1626 carved Jacobean pulpit with a tester and a 15th century screen. On the other hand, Butterfield's final stamp here is his own version of the Hertfordshire spike on top of the early 12th century tower.

Barnet

➤ Practically all the British counties can be traced right back to Saxon times, and, although the earliest actual mention of our county was as long ago as 1011, the first clear shape of Hertfordshire emerged only after the completion of Domesday Book in 1086.

Many geographical boundaries have been unchanged for centuries but in 1964 there were radical changes which caused Barnet to become part of Greater London. Potters Bar, in exchange, was taken into the county which did, purely from a physical point of view, make sense but to most people, including the County magazine, Barnet will always be part of Hertfordshire.

Barnet was in fact the gateway to the north, and with the Great North Road passing through it, not only were there many inns but early road improvement schemes were often centred on it with both Telford and McAdam being involved quite independently. Wadesmill may have been the place where the first turnpike gate was set up but there certainly was one here in 1712 operated by the Whetstone and Highgate Trust. Hidden away at the beginning of Ravenscroft Park, just off Wood Street and situated on the pavement opposite Grimsdyke House is a little stone block. The inscription carved on it reads – 'This stone was originally a Boundary Stone of Whetstone and Highgate Turnpike Trust which built Barnet Hill about 1823'. This little stone block has been preserved by its quiet anonymity but Barnet – really Chipping Barnet and Monken Hadley – has many architectural treasures to offer with quite a variety of old buildings still surviving in Wood Street despite the threat of the constant heavy traffic. St. John the Baptist's church, which dominates the hilltop junction appears to be mainly the 19th century enlargement of William Butterfield, but basically it is medieval and dates from circa 1420.

The oldest secular building, however, in this part of Barnet is Tudor Hall, which, originally the 'Free Grammar School of

Queen Elizabeth' of 1577, is situated in Wood Street almost opposite St. John's. Tudor Hall is likely to be missed by the visitor because since 1968 it has become incorporated into the Barnet College complex, but what cannot be overlooked is the interesting group of almshouses almost on top of one another further along Wood Street or just off Stapylton Road.

A brisk walk will take you past a mixed bag of 17th, 18th and 19th century cottages, all well preserved with No 20, now solicitor's offices, being one of the most interesting. After giving a glance in passing to the somewhat unusual architecture of the United Reformed church, the Ewen Hall next door, and Nos 51–53 opposite with their Ionic porch, Ravencroft Almshouses are reached. The almshouses were founded by James Ravencroft in 1679: an original '1679' date of stone under a lion is built into a modern gatepost with only the central archway with a gable above it being of the original date.

Almost next door are the six single storey almshouses founded by John Garrett in 1731, and the original plaque proclaiming this fact can be found on the side wall of the end almshouse together with another recording restorations in 1902 and 1982.

Then round the corner is the much more elaborate Leather-sellers Almshouses which were moved from Bishopsgate in the 19th century, although originally a foundation of 1544. Various restoration schemes have built them up to their present three ranges flanking a courtyard with a chapel on the north side facing fine double iron gates – also brought from Bishopsgate some 60 years ago.

These gates are generally kept locked but a small gateway beside the Lodge of 1861 in Stapylton Road, is in normal use. It is of interest, moreover, to note that a little further along Stapylton Road at the junction with The Drive, there stands what must be the oldest pillarbox in Barnet embossed with a curled cypher 'V.R.' which dates it from between 1887 and 1901.

Back on the Old North Road note that there are a number

of fine Georgian houses between the busy High Street and Monken Hadley but take particular note of Livingstone Cottage where David Livingstone, the missionary and explorer, lived in 1857. Round the corner is another group of six single storey almshouses founded by Roger Wilbraham in 1612 and they, together with the convent opposite, mark the beginning of the narrow approach to the 15th century St. Mary's church and the former tollgate to Hadley Common beyond.

St. Mary's church retains much of its 15th century appearance, much more so than St. John the Baptist back at the hilltop where, as already mentioned, the 19th century is more prominent. The 15th century appearance of St. Mary's at Monken Hadley is enhanced by the rare copper beacon on the stair turret on the top of the tower. Pevsner maintains that it is only of the 18th century, but it is said to have been one of those lit to warn of the approach of the Spanish Armada in 1588 – a much more romantic story but, whatever the truth of the matter, it has no rival in the county.

Between the church and the former tollgate are two pretty Gothic cottages but the whole of this little enclave, despite the constant through traffic, is full of architectural interest.

Back on the main road, the former A1 and now A1000, at what is known as Hadley Highstone is the 17th century King William IV inn and a few yards to the north is an obelisk which was erected in 1740 to recall the Battle of Barnet, on Easter Sunday 1471, when Warwick 'The Kingmaker' was slain by the forces of the triumphant Edward IV.

Bayford

➤ The church of St. Mary only dates from 1870, built on the site of two earlier churches and not of too great interest although a number of brasses and other memorials were transferred including a 15th century font.

In the churchyard lies buried William Yarrell, a naturalist whose books on fishes and birds were the best of their kind at the time. He was born in 1784 just four years before the founding of The Linnean Society in 1788, now the world's oldest learned body devoted to biology and natural history, which celebrated its bi-centenary in January 1988 with a set of postage stamps. Yarrell became the Society's treasurer and remained a vice-president until he died in 1856 to be buried in his mother's village.

In the middle of the 18th century the estate passed into the hands of the Baker family, who since 1757 were responsible for much to be seen in the parish, including the church and the great house of Bayfordbury with its long facade of 25 bays. It is now part of Hatfield Polytechnic but it still stands in grounds famous for its cedar trees, some dating back two centuries.

Bengeo

➤ To all intents and purposes Bengeo is part of the borough of Hertford with Holy Trinity, built only in 1855, being the official parish church. But Bengeo justifies its place here because of St. Leonard's, one of the oldest buildings in the county and certainly, arguably, the oldest, although now former, parish church. St. Leonard's is a rare example of a virtually intact early 12th century Norman church and complete with an apse – one of only three in the county.

It is used for services on occasion during the summer but it is well worth obtaining a key from one of the cottages nearby if only to examine the early 13th century wall painting of Christ being taken down from the Cross. This painting of the Deposition of Christ to the left of the simple chancel arch (which has the face of a man on one capital) was only uncovered in 1938, and is one of the finest of the various wall paintings still to be seen in the county.

Benington

◣ Along with Westmill, Benington is the epitome of the English Village, still more or less unspoilt notwithstanding its closeness to Stevenage. Timber-framed cottages (some with overhangs), The Bell Inn, the pond and St. Peter's church all encircle the village green with the manor house, just as it should be, in its rightful place near the churchyard to keep a benevolent eye on the feudal scene.

Not much more than a hamlet now, Benington has a long history. It was once the seat of the Saxon Kings of Mercia and Bertulf held a council here in 850 to discuss what to do about the invading Danes.

The Lordship Folly at Benington

31

Much later in medieval times, it was the Benstedes who became the lords of the manor and lived in a castle, the site of the present Georgian manor house. There are fragments of the old castle remaining although it was pulled down in 1212, and a folly in the shape of a Norman gatehouse was constructed out of remnants by a landscape gardener in 1832. The folly and the attractive gardens are open to the public at certain times of the year.

The 13th century sedilia in the chancel are the earliest pieces in the church but the main interest lies in the north chancel chapel and the arches with their fine stonework linking the chancel to the chapel. There are intriguing corbels including the head of a woman wearing a wimple on the arches, and beneath one arch the tomb of Sir John Benstede and his wife Petronilla, who built the chapel in 1330. Another Benstede and his lady lie under another arch. A screen, a font of Barnack Stone dating from the 14th century, and some original seating of 15th century are all of interest, but do not miss St. Michael who has been slaying the dragon in a niche over the entrance of the south porch for at least 650 years!

Berkhamsted

➤ An excellent little book *A Short History of Berkhamsted* by Percy Birtchnell gives the full story of this ancient town where William the Conqueror accepted the Crown of England from the defeated Saxon nobles, so what to look for that is 'hidden'?

It must be stressed that, although there probably was some form of Saxon stronghold before the events of 1066, it was only later that Robert, Earl of Mortain who was the Conqueror's half-brother, built the castle here and of that only the motte and bailey remain. The masonry which survives, now under the control of English Heritage, is thought to date from 1155–65 when Thomas a Becket held the castle as Chancellor. During Richard II's reign (1377–1399) Geoffrey Chaucer was Clerk of the Works but there is little evidence that he ever actually visited the castle. It is unfortunate that the railway cuts the castle off completely from the town – it would have enhanced the overall picture.

The oldest buildings in the town are practically opposite one another – Incent's House on the south side of the High Street and The Court House by St. Peter's church on the other side of the road. John Incent, later Dean of St. Paul's, lived in this half-timbered house of the 16th century (which is now a restaurant) and founded Berkhamsted School in 1541. The now famous public school can still point with pride to the original building of 1544 in Castle Street. The author Graham Greene was a pupil here when his father was headmaster.

The timber-framed Court House, inconspicuously tucked away is also of the 16th century, and was at one time where the Borough Court was held. It has been carefully preserved and is useful for church activities. St. Peter's church, at the top of Castle Street, is one of the biggest in the county with several restorations over the centuries in its history culminating in one between 1956 and 1960. There are many brasses and monuments including several to the Incent family and one to John Sayer, Charles II's chief cook, who died in 1681 and in his will left money for an almshouse, 'consisting of twelve rooms, designed for the habitation of six poor widows'. The almshouses, somewhat precariously, still stand in the High Street near the main road junction.

The east window of the church is a memorial to the poet William Cowper who was born in the town in 1731 when his father was rector, and his baptism is recorded in the register. He had his jolly periods – witness the poem *John Gilpin* – but his life was a sad one. Arthur Mee writes: 'His gentle spirit was invincibly humane, and yet his life was cursed by doubts about his soul. It is one of the tragedies of genius that this man who was so kind, so gentle that he could not hurt a fly, was driven insane by the thought that God would punish him.' He may have had his periods of 'melancholia' or, as we would call it today, 'mental breakdown' but he has left in common usage the expressions 'variety is the (very) spice of life' and 'the cups that cheer but not inebriate'.

Also near the road junction is the Victorian Town Hall which was built in 1860 after the Elizabethan Market House was destroyed by fire six years earlier. This is a building which, like many another, was threatened by re-development but has been saved as a notable piece of Victorian architecture.

Ashridge may be your next port of call so, after driving up the road past the castle to Berkhamsted Common and at the T-junction before turning left, note the memorial to the men of The Inns of Court Regiment who trained hereabouts during the First World War.

Bishops Stortford

➤ Being a well-documented town with a Town Trail issued by the Local History Society, obtainable from the museum, which gives not only a route round the old streets, but also fascinating information about the town's history, what can possibly be hidden in what was called Storteford in Domesday Book? After the Conquest William took the town for himself and built the original Norman church and Waytemore Castle before giving it to the Bishop of London – hence the name today.

Precious little masonry remains but the Waytemore Castle motte is a fine survival of a motte and bailey castle. The bailey has been completely incorporated into what is now The Castle Gardens and, although there are no defenders now, you must brave the traffic dangers of The Causeway before climbing the steps to make your own conquest of the 42 feet high motte.

The present St. Michael's church of circa 1400 still has the font of circa 1150 made for the old church, but the most exciting find is the 18 misericords in the choir stalls – like Anstey and Stevenage, an unusual feature in a parish church. The pulpit, which was made for £5 in 1658, has a fold down floor to raise up short preachers and there are all kinds of rustic characters as well as angels on the corbels in the aisles with the Apostles in the nave. The screen is original work of the 15th century although the vaulting on the top was added in 1885. I must record that the church guide is one of the most detailed that I have encountered in a parish church anywhere.

There are many old inns in the town and in particular, note one of the oldest The Boar's Head, which is directly opposite the church. Built in the late 16th century or early 17th century, it is a good example of timber and plaster building but, curiously, omitted by Pevsner.

The former Corn Exchange of 1828 had fallen into disuse by 1964 but, after a public outcry, was saved from demolition by being turned into offices and shops. There is much else to see in the town, and it is all detailed in the Trail but it must not be forgotten that this was the birthplace of Cecil Rhodes.

The Revd. Francis Rhodes, who has a window to his memory in St. Michael's, moved to South Road and his son, Cecil, was born there in 1853. He was educated in the town but, after suffering poor health as a youth, he was sent to Africa because it was thought that the open air life might benefit him. It made a man of him physically and he became an Empire Builder. As head of the De Beers organisation he amassed a large fortune and became Prime Minister of the Cape Legislature in 1890. He was responsible for forming the British South Africa Company in 1889 which occupied areas which were renamed Rhodesia after him. He died in 1902 and his birthplace was officially opened as a museum in 1938: it presents a fascinating panorama of Rhodes' life and his activities in what was Rhodesia and South Africa.

Boreham Wood

The complete entry in my little 1903 guidebook is 'Boreham Wood, 1¼ miles from Elstree, is a large and prettily situated hamlet', but it is Boreham Wood that is now

Big Brother, largely populated by London overspill. The film industry stretching back as far as 1900, is still here and not at Elstree itself, although much of the production is by foreign companies renting studio space. British success today is highlighted through television – Albert Square for the *East Enders* location is in the BBC Centre here, and open days are arranged from time to time!

'The hamlet' itself now sports a variety of buildings – District Offices, swimming pool, churches of all denominations and, horror of horrors, a tall tower block which together with large housing estates, finally turned the place into a 'town'.

Bourne End

◆ Situated just outside the designated area when the postwar boundaries of Hemel Hempstead were drawn up, Bourne End escaped the impact of the huge housing estates which sprang up all over the New Town. Bourne End lies astride the busy A41, and if you blink or yawn (as a passenger, of course!) you may miss it, and that would be a mistake.

Sir George Gilbert Scott, more famous for his Albert Memorial and St. Pancras Station, or, more correctly, the Midland Grand Hotel in front of the station, designed the little church of St. John in 1854. He added a variation of the 'spike', the thin recessed spires in various shapes and sizes which are a characteristic of the county's churches, although these are usually to be found on the top of towers. Here, on the roof of the east end of the nave, and very reminiscent of an old-fashioned candle extinguisher, is an embodiment of the alternative name for the 'spike' – the 'snuffer'.

Between 1971 and 1974 a hotel was built incorporating the former 19th century watermill, and at first it was called The Watermill Hotel. The waterwheel is preserved within the fabric of the hotel and originally was depicted on the sign by the highway. Sadly, after the hotel was taken over in 1982, the hotel was unimaginatively renamed The Moat House like the rest of the controlling Group. Big Business apparently has no soul!

Bovingdon

➤ Like neighbouring Flaunden, Bovingdon was once part of the parish of Hemel Hempstead, but now has become a suburb outpost of the expanding new town, a process which was accelerated by the building of the wartime airfield. The approach to Bovingdon up Box Lane takes you past the oddly-sited golf course, seemingly climbing vertically at one hole, but when the top is reached make sure that you take the first left turning. If you do not you will drive past what the airfield has been converted into – a Youth Custody Centre, renamed The Mount.

In the village the most conspicuous object is a well built to perpetuate the memory of the Hon. Granville D. Ryder, late of Westbrook Hay (see Boxmoor) who died in 1879. The dedication is carved on the four sides of the pump which is well preserved – it was being reroofed with chestnut wood on my last visit to the village in 1988.

Church Street has some interesting cottages – elsewhere in the village little of interest. St. Lawrence's church itself was only built in 1845 on the site of a church which had stood since the Conquest. Although the lower part of the walls of the tower were incorporated the present pinnacled tower does not have the normal county look to it! Note inside the effigy of an armoured knight of circa 1400 from the old church, and outside the exceptionally large churchyard complete with ordered rows of clipped yew trees.

As you leave Bovingdon for Chipperfield the Rentstreet Barns and cottage cannot fail to catch the eye: 16th and 17th century and timber-framed.

Boxmoor

➤ Almost overwhelmed by, and part of, the borough of Hemel Hempstead, Boxmoor manages to retain a little individuality through having its own 19th century church of St. John and, of course, the Grand Union Canal meandering through what remains of the original 'moor'. The people of Boxmoor had the right to graze cattle and poultry on the moor, and several houses in the High Street still bear 'Rights of Pasture' plaques – a right which, in theory, still exists!

The Fishery Inn, despite the concrete bridge, still retains its fascination for photographers, especially if a gaily decorated narrowboat (correct name for the more humble 'barge') is going by manned by cruising holiday-makers. When I first came to know the area British Waterways narrowboats plied their trade carrying cargo – now it is all leisure activity.

Under the skew bridge carrying the main British Rail line to Glasgow, past Box Lane leading to Bovingdon is an inconspicuous entrance leading to what is now a private school – Westbrook Hay. It was from this early 19th century building that the Development Corporation watched over the growth of the New Town, but it had been the home of the Hon. Granville D. Ryder (see Bovingdon).

Practically opposite this school entrance and on what once was part of the moor, are two white stones which make up the supposed burial place of Robert Snooks, a highwayman hanged nearby. The story goes that, whilst being taken to the place of execution, he asked some villagers rushing by as to why they were hurrying. Unaware of his identity, they shouted back that 'We are going to see Snooks hung!' to which he replied 'Well, nothing will happen until I get there!'.

Bramfield

➤ Barely more than a hamlet, this little village has one great claim to fame: according to the chronicler Matthew Paris, the church of St Andrew was the first living of the Canterbury martyred St. Thomas a Becket, and his name heads the list of rectors. After entering the service of Henry II, he became Chancellor of England in 1155, and Archbishop of Canterbury in 1162. Henry's friendship turned to hatred when Becket resisted all attempts by Henry to bring the clergy under the jurisdiction of the royal courts. In 1170, after the King's injudicious outburst 'Are there none of the cowards eating my bread who will rid me of this turbulent priest?', four of his knights went to Canterbury and murdered the unfortunate Archbishop.

Restorations in 1840 destroyed nearly all traces of antiquity but the simple plan of chancel and nave remain unaltered from the original church of the 11th century and an earlier rebuilding in the 14th century. Note the two figures on either side of the south porch. A pond near the church is still called 'Becket's Pond' and the local tradition has it that Becket brewed his beer from it!

A well on the tiny green was the villagers' only source of water until piped water reached every house in 1937. The well was concreted over for safety at the time but in 1953 it became useful again with a new purpose. Now a plaque on it reads:

'To Commemorate Coronation of
H.M. Queen Elizabeth II
2nd June 1953
The village well house was
converted into a shelter'

Before leaving this microscopic village buy a stamp at the sub-post office – a former school, this thatched cottage is as picturesque a post office as you will find anywhere.

Braughing

➤ The mainly 15th century church in its picturesque setting across the river Quin must be one of the most photographed spots in the county but Brachinges at the time of the Domesday Book was already old. Systematic excavations have revealed an extensive Roman town just south of the present village (now pronounced Braffing) which existed between A.D. 80 and A.D. 350, and was second only to St. Albans in importance.

The village is virtually in two parts with the river cutting it in two although a ford provides the link. The B1368 from Puckeridge takes speeding motorists quickly along the High Street past The Gables which boasts it was built 'circa 1400' and they are quickly gone, but the best lies across the ford for the leisurely readers of this book.

Over the ford, past the village green keep left and there is then much to enjoy through just looking at the various buildings grouped around the church of St. Mary, and further in the square or market place, 16th and 17th century cottages, some timbered and some pargetted with overhanging upper storey, jostle for recognition with the Victorian 'tudor' cottage of timber and herringbone built in 1860.

It is all delightful and inside the church itself there is also much to see and savour.

The interior of the church, which has been described as 'sumptuous' is mainly of the 15th century although the chancel dates back to the 12th century. Angels help to hold up the nave roof at the feet of the roof trusses, and there are all kinds of decorated faces on the corbels. There are more angels in the aisles with more gargoyles on the embattled two-storeyed south porch and the tower holds a bell of 1562 which is the oldest in the county.

Away from the village are two places of interest. To the east on the very minor road linking the village with the A120, Upp Hall, now much altered but originally a Jacobean mansion, has an exceptionally large barn of late 16th century which is 140 feet long together with a 17th century building called 'The Granary'. To the west of the village, the other side of the A10, is Hamels Park with its lodges of 1783 (see Munden, Great and Little).

Breachwood Green

➤ Within the Kings Walden parish this hamlet is growing, so, despite being below the flight path to Luton airport, deserves a place for two other reasons.

Surrounded by bushes, derelict and standing abandoned as if rejected by the village, one of the county's few windmills still stands down a track. Back in the village, however, the 1904 Baptist chapel, with a quite extraordinary west front, topped by what Pevsner calls 'prominent ironmongery', holds a pulpit of 1658 from which John Bunyan used to preach. You will remember, of course, that 1658 was the date of the death of that other great Puritan, Oliver Cromwell.

Brent Pelham

➤ Tradition has it that both church and village were destroyed by fire during the reign of Henry I (1100–1135), hence the later coining of 'Brent' from 'Burnt'. Outside St. Mary's church in the centre of the village stand the old stocks and whipping post, one of a very few left in the county but one which seems to have been missed by Pevsner. The church generally is about 100 years younger than that at neighbouring Furneux Pelham but it has its spike on the embattled tower and commandment boards on either side of the nave. The original 14th century door is preserved alongside the new in the south porch but locally the church is famous for a tomb in the north wall.

This tomb, under a recess in the north wall, has a 13th century black marble slab elaborately decorated with the symbols of the four Evangelists, and in the centre a foliate cross inserted in a dragon's mouth, signifying the triumph of Christianity. The tomb also bears a figure in relief of an angel bearing to heaven a human soul in the shape of a small figure. The tomb is of an unknown person but over the centuries a legend has grown up locally about it being the tomb of Piers Shonks who, when medieval lord of the manor, supposedly slew a dragon. As the story was told and elaborated over the centuries, so did Shonks become a giant – or at least a mighty hunter.

Cussans relates that: 'It so happened that Shonks, when hunting in the forest, killed a dragon (shown on the tomb) which was under the immediate protection of the Devil who declared in revenge that he would possess Shonks at his death, whether buried within or without the church. It seems that Piers was too wily to be caught thus, and left directions in his will that he should be buried in the middle of the wall – neither within or without the church!'.

Opposite the church, Brent Pelham Hall may be glimpsed from the road but if you retrace your steps down the B1038 towards the Essex border, note the former early 17th century manor house of Beaches, although the ordnance map has it as 'Beeches'. Now a farm, its former importance can be judged by the huge outer chimneys but all the original panelling and mantlepieces were transferred to Brent Pelham Hall in the 19th century.

Less than a mile from Beaches Farm and even nearer to Essex, is what the Royal Commission calls an earthwork, possibly a medieval fishpond, which is called Shonk's Moat. Its very name helps to keep alive the legend of Piers Shonks whose exploits were extolled for centuries after his death in 1086, a date found painted on the back of the recess in the church although this is apparently only an 18th century inscription.

Brookmans Park

➤ Apparently a Garden Suburb which did not quite make it in size, Brookmans Park lies in the parish of North Mimms and is now a collection of 'very desirable residences', despite the nearness of the BBC transmitter masts beside what was the A1 now the A1000.

The Suburb is virtually built in the grounds of two former estates – Brookmans and Gobions – dating from the 16th century or earlier but both are long demolished, now with just the stables of Brookmans converted into a golf club-house. Gobions belonged to the More family until after the Civil War, and Sir Thomas More, the original 'Man for All Seasons' is reputed to have written *Utopia* while living there.

All that remains now is the Folly Arch at the junction of Swanley Bar Lane and Hawkshead Lane which was erected as an eye-catcher to the house in circa 1750. The designer seems to have been James Gibbs, better known for his work at Stowe and in Cambridge.

Broxbourne

➤ In Domesday Book as Brochesborne, Broxbourne in times past was a large parish containing 'the hamlet of Hoddesdon' but today the positions are reversed with Brox-bourne being a small portion of the Hoddesdon Urban District, although it has grown considerably in recent years.

The railway and the river Lea act as part of the county boundary with Essex, which fact has helped to make that part of the town a major centre of the Lea Valley Regional Park. Incidentally, the railway station was one of the first modern stations built after the Second World War on a different site to the old one.

Many old buildings have disappeared in recent years but when Broxbourne school was built in 1959, a large house of the 18th century was retained on the site. The best survivor, slightly further north, is the Monson Almshouses of 1728. The Monson family seat was Broxbournebury, the present building being of 19th century rebuilding of an earlier 16th century mansion. It is now a Special School.

The parish church of St. Augustine, nicely situated by the New river has an unusual north chapel with a vestry as a second storey. Around the top of the parapet to this is an inscription 'in honor a ye Trenete the yere of our Lord God 1522' put up by the man who built it, 'Syr Wylliam Say Knyct'. There is also a south chapel built in 1476 by Robert Stowell who went on to build St. Margaret's, Westminster.

The south porch doorway of circa 1645 is what has been called 'an exuberant piece of work' with an 'agnus dei' over the arch and above that a segmental pediment with a shield over it. Above the actual door into the church in the south porch is a plaque which reads: 'Arise ye dead and come to judgement'.

There is a 12th century font of Purbeck marble but the interior is chiefly notable for the monuments. The usual tributes to local knights but perhaps the most interesting are those to persons with more familiar names: Edward Christian, who died in 1823, was the elder brother of Fletcher Christian who led the mutiny on the *Bounty*, and John McAdam who died in 1836 after spending the last years of his life in Broxbourne, has a tablet commemorating that he was 'the great Improver of the British Roads'. McAdam lived at Montague House in Hoddesdon from 1823 until his death in 1836. He is said to have described the coming of the railway as his 'Waterloo' – he could in no way have forecast the mighty motorways of today as opposed to the reduction of the railway network!

Buntingford

➤ After many years of frustration and much campaigning, a bypass taking the A1 round this little town opened in 1987, so now it is much easier to take a longer look at what is hidden – hopefully the lorries heading for the huge warehouse of the well-known supermarket chain will no longer clog up the long High Street, part of Roman Ermine Street.

Although it was built by the Romans, Ermine Street was first mentioned in land records in 1185 and Edward III granted a market charter in 1360, but my Little Guide of 1903 says 'Little of historic importance is to be gleaned in the town. . . '. There is, of course, much local history but there can be no disputing the rest of the sentence, 'but a ramble from end to end is interesting by reason of the many quaint inns and cottages, of all ages and styles, which meet the eye at every turn'.

The best almshouses – and I hasten to add architecturally – in the county are at the southern end of the High Street, founded by Bishop Seth Ward in 1685. Seth Ward was born in Aspenden in 1618, educated at Buntingford Grammar School (now a building called Layston Court) and went on to become Bishop of Salisbury, an original member of the Royal Society and Chancellor of the Order of the Garter. He never forgot his humble origins, and so founded what is an excellent example of an open quadrangle almshouse, still retaining the name of 'Hospital' – as the lintel inscription testifies in his honour.

Also near the almshouses is the covered pump or well erected to commemorate the Jubilee of Queen Victoria but further north on the same side is a public turret clock which dates back to the 16th century. This little one-handed clock, over a covered way between the old Angel Inn and a house rebuilt in 1906, contains a bell that until recent years was used to call Buntingford to church and is still tolled at the death of a monarch. A good view of the back can be had from the car park.

By the side of the river Rib on the way to the still standing but abandoned church at Layston is a brick lock-up, in poor state when last seen but hopefully still intact. St. Bartholomew's was the church for the settlement of Layston but when the medieval settlement was deserted in favour of Buntingford growing around the main road, the congregation found it became a chore to go to church so St. Peter's, previously a chapel at ease, was built between 1614 and 1626 at the southern end of Buntingford, a stone's throw from where the almshouses were built later in the century.

Nothing of note except that an apse was added in 1899, completely out of keeping and certainly not to be counted among the three Norman apses mentioned elsewhere in this book!

Bushey

◣ Bushey, like Gaul, is divided into two parts – Bushey and Bushey Heath – and was at one time just a charming village with a pond, and a heath with fine views over London. Now it is virtually just an extension of the urban sprawl of Watford with much of the heath built over, albeit some of the houses are, in the words of the ubiquitous estate agents, very desirable residences indeed!

Despite all that, the pond is still there right by the church of St. James in what is called the core of the old village, opposite some cottages which have a little gentle floral pargetting on each. The church goes back to the 13th century, although there was extensive restoration in 1871 by Gilbert Scott who added the aisles and a north porch. Retained were the Jacobean pulpit with its tester and, instead of a chancel arch, a 15th century beam supporting a plastered partition, on which are painted the Royal Arms of Queen Anne.

In the churchyard are interred the remains of Sir Hubert von Herkomer, a German who settled in Bushey, and founded an Art School in what was then what he called a 'sleepy picturesque village'. This is not the place to reflect on his influence on the Art World but he certainly was an influence on the little community. After founding his Art School in 1883, Herkomer commissioned an American, H. H. Richardson, to build him an extraordinary house which was completed in 1894, although Richardson himself died in 1886. The house looked like a mountain schloss, especially after his father *and* grandfather had enriched it with carvings. It was called 'Lululaund' after his first wife but was pulled down in 1939 – that is, all but the front entrance which Pevsner says 'must at all costs be preserved' because it is the only European work by the best American architect of the 19th century. You can see this front in Melbourne Road where it, somewhat incongruously, fronts the hut of the Bushey branch of the British Legion.

All around the vicinity of Melbourne Road are reminders of Herkomer: at the top end are the film studios he built in 1914, now converted into offices, and opposite is another of his residences now the offices of Bushey Colour Laboratories. Herkomer pulled his Art Studio down in 1912 and there is now a Rose Garden open to the public with just a fountain to remind us of this remarkable man.

Bygrave

Henry III granted a charter to hold a market here back in the 13th century but there is little evidence now that it was ever a market town – that dignity probably drifted away in later centuries across the Cat Ditch to its bigger neighbour Ashwell.

At the Manor Farm, in this now very small village, are ditches and banks which are perhaps the defences of a British tribe before the Romans marched down the nearby Icknield Way (now A505). If there is any doubt whether they are as old as that it is certainly known that the ditches were converted into moats at the end of the 14th century as a defensive measure by Sir John Thornbury.

The little half octagonal turret to a wooden bell cote on the outside of the west end of the little church of St. Margaret demands notice but there are several treasures inside despite there being only nave and chancel. A Norman south doorway although the porch itself is only of the 18th century, an octagonal 15th century font, some 15th century benches with poppyheads, even some Roman bricks in the nave, all add to the interest. The best, however, is a great rarity – attached to the pulpit is a 17th century hourglass stand made of wrought iron.

Cheshunt

My little 1903 Guide separates Cheshunt and Waltham Cross, although the Royal Commission Inventory, Arthur Mee and others have pushed them together, so let us keep them apart because they do seem to have become two distinct localities. Sadly what the Little Guide says of Cheshunt, 'a large parish which contains much of interest', no longer holds water because so much has been destroyed or demolished. Of Lord Burghley's Theobalds Palace, accepted by James I in exchange for the Old Hatfield House, there is virtually only a few bricks left, even of what was called Old Palace House built on the site after the demolition of Theobalds after Charles I's execution. Another loss was the 15th century Great House of Cheshunt, one of Cardinal Wolsey's homes, which conveniently got burned down in 1965 and so made way for a large housing complex!

There is still the successor to Lord Burghley's old palace, Theobalds Park built in 1763 and much added to by the brewing family Meux in the 19th century. It is now an Educational Centre but in the grounds is the much neglected, but by no means forgotten, Temple Bar which was erected as an entrance to Theobalds Park by Sir Henry Meux in 1888. One of Wren's masterpieces in a minor key, it was completed in 1672 and, until 1878, was a gateway to the City of London: in that year it was taken down as a traffic hazard. Plans have been announced that it is to be returned to The City to rest in the shadow of Wren's major masterpiece, St. Paul's Cathedral but, as I write of activity there is none.

So, what else is left? Older than all those which are no more, is the church of St. Mary which was built between 1418 and 1448 although much restored in 1872 and 1892. There is a 12th century font and in the churchyard a Saxon stone coffin.

Opposite the church is a path from what is called Churchgate and this leads to what was the original Cheshunt village and there still stands the Dewhurst Charity School of 1640. Nearby is the Old Parsonage, partly 16th century, where 'Tumbledown Dick', Oliver Cromwell's son Richard died in 1712 after living quietly as 'Mr. Clarke' for 30 years in the house of one Sergeant Pengelly.

Retracing one's steps to Churchgate, there is the former Bishop's College – you will find that this complex is now the Council Offices of Broxbourne District Council, and much addicted to red embellishment. However, one last antiquity may restore one's hope that all has not been swept away – there are 17th century almshouses in the main road at Turners Hill directly opposite a garage with the usual riot of signs and colours.

Childwick Green

━ Although Childwick Green is not a village in the true meaning of the word it certainly deserves its place here, if only because they had to promote a special prize for it in the annual Best Kept Village Competition! Neither Harpenden nor St. Albans but about midway between the two, this beautifully kept little 'village' with its well on the green used to be where the Childwickbury estate workers lived. Now the 17th century mansion, for many years the home of the Joel family, belongs to a film director, the estate is split up and the houses are privately owned.

The little chapel of St. Mary was built in 1867 by Gilbert Scott, the lodge on the main road only dates from 1897, but at daffodil time and rhododendron time people come from far and wide just to enjoy the profusion of colour.

Chipperfield

➤ When the Royal Commission's Inventory was made in 1910, Chipperfield was shrugged off as 'a hamlet' 2 miles west of Kings Langley, so much of the village today is comparatively modern, although the very popular Two Brewers was a favourite training centre in the 19th century for prize-fighters and dates back to the 16th century. Just to the north of the Two Brewers is the Pale Farm House, a 16th century building with an overhanging upper storey. It takes its name from having been just outside the 'pale' of the Royal Park at Kings Langley.

On the roadside by the extensive common is the normal village war memorial but past the inn, past the old flint school now converted into flats, is the village hall which stands opposite St. Paul's church built 1837. On the wall is the sad plaque which reads: 'This Clubhouse was given to the Village of Chipperfield by Samuel and Elizabeth Black-well of the Manor House in memory of their sons Charles and William Gordon and the men of Chipperfield who gave their lives for their country in the Great War 1914–1918'.

The manor house lies on the far side of the common but on the common itself is The Apostle's Pond surrounded by 12 lime trees representing the Twelve Apostles. St. Paul's church is unremarkable but it has a lychgate at the north entrance.

Chorley Wood

➤ Not much hidden here and they are very proud of their 200 acre common which provides many recreational facilities including a 9-hole golf course.

There are a few old cottages and farms to show that Chorley Wood was, indeed, once a village, but mainly it is a result of the growth of Metroland between the wars. The Council Offices are now housed in Chorley Wood House and its grounds are now a public park on the other side of the road to the common.

In one corner of the common is the cricket ground, and nearby is the mid-Victorian church of Christ Church with a stone reredos and pulpit, all by the architect of the building.

Between Chorley Wood West and Chorley Wood Bottom is Shire Lane where the famous architect Charles Voysey built himself a house called 'The Orchard' in 1900, and on the Haddon Road, a turning off Shire Lane there is, despite what the Thames and Chiltern Tourist Board brochure about Three Rivers District says, an Edward VIII pillar box.

Clothall

━━ Clothall lies just off the Baldock to Buntingford road which slices across the wide open spaces of north Herts. It is virtually only a hamlet now with reputedly less houses today than a century or so ago.

There is no school either but a house to the east of the church started life as one in the middle of the 19th century. There must have been a lot of children once. In the church there is a 16th century brass in honour of Ann Bramfield who bore 16 children – no doubt as so often happened, many died in infancy.

There are two pre-Reformation bells in the tower of St. Mary's, which also has the 14th century porch set into it. The wooden door is original, pitted with hundreds of holes made when putting up church notices over the ages, but do not miss the name 'John Warren' facing into the church – probably the craftsman who made it in the 14th century.

There are low box pews here with poppyhead benchends, and a 12th century font of Purbeck marble but the chief glory is the east window filled with a variety of birds above the heads of Christ, St. Mary Magdalene and the four evangelists, all in glass of the 14th century and 15th century. The head of St. Mary Magdalene is reputed to have come from the chapel of an old leper hospital nearby which was suppressed in 1547.

Before leaving this tiny place take note of the former rectory just south of the church. Now called Clothall House, it is a typical Georgian rectory of the period which no cleric could possibly maintain today.

Codicote

Recorded in Domesday Book as Cuthering Coton, Codicote has a long history. It has survived through many centuries, when other villages virtually disappeared for ever after the Black Death, because it stood on the route of the old Great North Road. Despite that, and after being granted a charter for a fair giving it the status of a small market town, it has remained a village although now mainly a dormitory for the surrounding towns, or even further afield, with a population in excess of 3,000.

The former 'George & Dragon' at Codicote

Right in the middle of the village stands a fine half-timbered hostelry which is now called the 'As you like it' Restaurant, but ask any of the local inhabitants and they will refer to it as The George and Dragon which it was for many years, even centuries past. This building dates back to the late 16th century and it stands on the site of what was probably the oldest licensed premises in the county, at one time called The Greyhound, with records reaching at least as far back as the year 1279.

In complete contrast to this is Node Court between Codicote and Knebworth, a most unusual sight in the countryside. It was originally built in 1927, believe it or not, as a cowshed to fulfil an American's ideas on modern dairy farming: it is now partly luxury home and partly offices.

Mention must be made of the barn converted into a house at the beginning of the Wheathampstead road along with some other modern houses with names which reflect the existence of a forge on the site in time past, but Bury Lane is where much of the remaining interest lies.

On the left is the 1857 village school which is now helping to house that 3,000 plus: further along on the right is The Bury, itself built circa 1655 and a fine example of the period. Now no longer in private hands, it provides sheltered housing for pensioners in purpose-built extensions and bungalows.

Once at the centre of the medieval village, St. Giles' church stands on the edge of the village, and although it has a Victorian look about it because of drastic restoration in 1853, dates right back to the 13th century. There is a contemporary lancet window, a 15th century tower arch and a Jacobean pulpit, but there is a thought-provoking curiosity back in the churchyard near the gate. A wooden graveboard reads:

'In memory of John Gootheridge
Who died October 30th 1824. In the 79th year of his Age.
Reburied a Week Later'.

The story is apparently as follows. After John Gootheridge

was buried for the first time, his grave was opened by body snatchers. Before they could make off with the body they were disturbed and fled, leaving the corpse on the ground in the open! As a consequence a second burial took place a week later.

Coleman Green

━ Coleman Green, a tiny hamlet half-way along a very narrow lane, marked on the OS map as 'Roman Road', between Sandridge and Water End, would not qualify to be included here except for one very important item. As Arthur Mee puts it 'It must surely be the only place in England that has a chimney stack for a monument'. John Bunyan, the author of *Pilgrim's Progress* often preached in the county and this preserved chimney stack has a stone tablet on it which reads 'John Bunyan is said by tradition to have preached and occasionally have lodged in the cottage of which this chimney was a part'.

Two or three cottages, and a popular public house, naturally called The John Bunyan make up the hamlet but at Water End stands the Jacobean manor house right by the river Lea, and controversy still rages as to whether or not it was the birthplace of Sarah Jennings, the future Duchess of Marlborough. It is certainly where she spent much of her childhood.

Colney Heath

━ There certainly is a heath here, once the haunt of highwaymen, but the parish really includes not only the village of Colney Heath itself but also a number of hamlets including Tyttenhanger and Smallford. Although there is nothing of great interest in Colney Heath with a church

Bunyan's Pot at Coleman Green

dating from only 1845, there are interesting cottages of various centuries in Smallford and Sleapshyde.

There is still a coal duty post in Coursers Road, and crossing the heath on the way to London Colney (both places deriving their names from the river Colne which flows through both) there is a tower mill which has been cleverly incorporated into the Old Mill House.

Further along the same B556 road there is a turning to the fine red brick mansion of Tyttenhanger Hall of circa 1650 which is now the offices of a well known firm of architects. This house was built on the site of one built in 1410 and the country retreat of the Abbots of St Albans. It was granted to Sir Thomas Pope, the founder of Trinity College Oxford, after the Dissolution of the Monasteries and here he entertained Henry VIII.

Cottered

A large village lying along the A507 between Baldock and Buntingford, and in medieval times was on a pilgrim route from the Midlands to the shrine of our Lady of Walsingham in Norfolk. This could account for the huge wall painting of St. Christopher on the north wall of the aisleless nave of St. John the Baptist's church: apparently touched up when I saw it, it is most vivid and Cottered is worth visiting for that alone.

The church has a 14th century embattled tower with, although bigger than many, undoubtedly a spike. Note also the little quatrefoil window in the chancel above a blocked-up door (look outside as well) and an unusual font of Derbyshire Marble of 1739.

Opposite the church is a farmhouse known as The Lordship, complete with moat fragment and dovecote. This building is reputed to be the oldest inhabited house in the county but its front door of circa 1450–80 is now in America!

Cromer

➤ Cromer is, in most handbooks, covered by Ardeley of which parish it is, indeed, a part, but I feel that it deserves an entry of its own.

Its chief claim to fame is the post mill, the only one in a county with very few windmills. Probably 18th century, although it is recorded that there has been a mill on this site for over 650 years, this mill ceased to function some time in 1930. It was restored by the Herts Building Preservation Trust between 1967 and 1970 when new sails were also fitted but winds and hurricanes have forced their removal again: the mill certainly remains a landmark!

In the hamlet itself take note, as you pass through, of Cromer Farm, a particularly attractive 16th century half-timbered farmhouse with overhangs and gables which can be glimpsed through an opening between two similarly aged barns.

Croxley Green

➤ Arthur Mee wrote in 1939 it is 'a rapidly growing place by a big green on a hill near Watford'; now that hill is covered with houses and Croxley Green appears 'trapped' between Watford and Rickmansworth. Fortunately not completely trapped because that big green is still there for all to enjoy, with an escape to Sarratt and Chipperfield over the M25!

At the southern end of the green is another of those Victorian churches which appear quite characterless, but it has got an unusual round tower. In a road off Scots Hill there is a tower windmill which has been converted into a house (and shown on the OS map), and there are some period houses at the north end of the green but the jewel in the crown lies between the railway and the river Gade. This is a medieval tithe barn and reputed to be the second largest in the whole country.

The barn was built between 1396 and 1401 when the Abbey of St. Albans owned the manor of Rickmansworth and used it to store tithe produce. It measures 101 feet by 40 feet, and consists of five weather-boarded bays with a porch on the eastern side of the central bay through the doors of which could be driven a fully laden hay cart.

The barn was purchased by the County Council in 1973, and is occasionally open to the public. It stands in the grounds of Croxley Hall Farm, which formerly was called Croxley Manor House and in 1557 belonged to Dr. Caius, who was educated at Gonville College, Cambridge. He later endowed and greatly enlarged the college which became, as now, Gonville and Caius (pronounced 'keys') College.

Cuffley

➤ The modern church of St. Andrew, which won a Civic Trust Award when it was built in 1968, cannot fail to be the dominating feature of the residential area of this otherwise architecturally uninteresting commuter-belt village. However, do not let the geometrical patterns of this church prevent you from taking a look at another new church built for the Baptists a year or two earlier, and barely 200 yards away.

Cuffley has a fine Country Park called The Great Wood between the village and the old A1 but Cuffley will always be remembered as the place where a Zeppelin fell after being shot down by Lieut. Leefe Robinson in September 1916. He became famous that Sunday morning by breaking up the plans of the biggest Zeppelin raid of the First World War. He had already unsuccessfully attacked one of 14 Zeppelins when he shot one down over Cuffley, for which exploit he was awarded the VC. He lived through the rest of the war, but by a cruel stroke of fate, died from influenza on the last day of 1918 – just a few weeks after the Armistice.

Between Cuffley and Cheshunt is Goffs Oak with a church of 1862, and amid the estate development and glass-houses, there are some 19th century buildings with rare old pillar boxes in the garden of one of them.

Datchworth

➤ On Datchworth Green, the centre of a little area made up of several hamlets all blessed with a 'Green' in the name and a much-favoured locality, stands a grim relic of the past. This is a whipping post surrounded by an iron grill which has been carefully preserved and it bears the legend 'This Whipping Post was last known to be used on July 27 1665 when two vagabonds were publicly flogged here'.

South of here, in Bramfield Woods, there is another post by the roadside inscribed with the words 'Clibbon's Post'. Clibbon was a highwayman who might have been glad of just being whipped instead of being shot after being caught in the act of robbing a local farmer. His death, in December 1782, was a cause of general rejoicing and he is reputedly buried under this post. There is or should be a plaque which reads 'Here continues to rot the body of Walter Clibbon who, with his sons, robbed and ill-treated many persons in this neighbourhood. Please do not deface this'.

The church of All Saints at the north end of the parish, in Datchworth proper, has a spire like an inverted ice-cream cone and, standing at the highest point of the area, can be seen from quite a few miles away. The nave, which is out of the perpendicular, is of the 12th century with various additions of later periods including the lower part of the tower which is 15th century: note the blocked up door at the base. Also worthy of note are the coffin covers and 'bedhead' graveboards in the churchyard, whilst inside is a coffin lid with a foliated cross of circa 1300 in a recess.

Digswell

➤ 6,000 'navvies' worked on it for three years from 1848–1850, some 5,000,000 bricks made locally composed the structure with 40 arches and what resulted was the massive Digswell railway viaduct carrying the main line on its way from Kings Cross to Edinburgh.

Digswell is now part of Welwyn Garden City but it earns its own place for a variety of reasons not least because, despite the ever present viaduct, it is a delightful village with some half-timbered cottages, not at all dominated by Big Brother.

The other two reasons are Digswell House and St. John's church standing proudly together amid the housing estates. St. John's dates back to the 12th century but many alterations over the years culminated in an extension in 1962. A curiosity to be found in the north aisle is some tracery together with the figure of a dove dating from circa 1290, but do not overlook the memorials on behalf of all the Australian officers nursed at Digswell House (built 1807) in the First World War.

Eastwick

➤ Confronted by the whole might of Harlow across the river Stort in Essex, this little village neatly arranged around a loop off the A414, defies all attempts at change. It is possible that the planners might have considered adding Eastwick to Essex, to be later absorbed into the then infant New Town, when they made boundary changes in 1964 but the river and the railway no doubt combined to keep Esteuuiche, as it was in Domesday Book, just where it always has been in Hertfordshire.

Note that many of the cottages are mid-Victorian and dated, because many of them were built in the 1860s by the Hodgson family who held both Eastwick and Gilston Park from 1850 until 1886. They were estate cottages at that time but now even the school which the Hodgsons built in 1884 has become a filling station!

The church of St. Botolph, the only one dedicated to that saint in the county now that the church at Shenley is a private house, is another of those churches kept locked with no indication as to where the key can be obtained. The church was rebuilt in 1872 but there is still an elaborate 13th century chancel arch resting on shafts of Purbeck marble. Under the tower is an effigy of the same date which is encased in carved chain-mail which is considered to be an unusually perfect illustration of the armour of that period, complete with long surcoat and with a long shield.

As I turned away from the locked church with regret, I noticed that there are gargoyles near the top of the tower to take away the rain water – this was some consolation to me because this is not mentioned in any guidebook I have read about this place.

Elstree

Elstree used to be known, at least to photographers, for its group of weatherboarded cottages on Watling Street opposite the church, and also, erroneously, for its film studios. The cottages now have gone with unexciting flats built on the site and it was at Boreham Wood, admittedly in the parish of Elstree, where the British dream factory *really* was operating.

Elstree is still a village, more widely known now for its small aerodrome and its connections with the Aldenham Country Park (see Aldenham). The church of St. Nicholas, largely a creation of 1853, actually has bits and pieces dating back to the original 15th century building, and inside there is an octagonal font of the 15th century together with an alabaster monument of 1603 to one Olive Buck.

In the churchyard are the graves of two victims of murder

– Martha Ray, shot in 1779 by a man she had rejected, and William Weare, whose murder, by a one-time associate, became a cause célèbre in 1823.

Martha Ray, born in the village in 1746, became the mistress of the 4th Earl of Sandwich by whom she is said to have had nine children. While living at Hinchingbrooke in Huntingdon, a young man, James Hackman, fell in love with her in 1772 but she persistently refused his offers of marriage. Finally, after seven years, he waited for her outside Covent Garden Theatre one night and shot her dead. He was hanged at Tyburn, and her gravestone can be found a few yards from the east end of the church. William Weare's grave is unmarked.

Essendon

This little hilltop village of little cottages appears in its remoteness to be in the depths of the country with the 17th century Salisbury Crest Inn adding to the illusion. But remote it is not. Being within easy reach not only of Hatfield and the county town, and also near to London, the large mansions in the immediate neighbourhood have all become desirable and useful properties.

Early 19th century Essendon Place is now The Eastern Electricity Staff Training College, whilst Bedwell Park, at one time the home of Samuel Whitbread who devoted his life to social reform, is now the Hatfield and London Country Club, an attractive golf club. A third large mansion is Camfield Place, where an uncle of Beatrix Potter lived with whom she stayed on many occasions when she was young. Camfield Place is now the home of Barbara Cartland, an author of a different type of romance.

In September 1916 the church of St. Mary was bombed by the German Zeppelin which was later that night brought down by Lieutenant Leefe Robinson VC at Cuffley, but luckily the bomb failed to damage the black basalt Wedgwood font which had been given to the church by Mary, one of Samuel Whitbread's sisters in 1778. It is a very precious relic, the only other one is at Cardington in Bedfordshire also given by the Whitbreads, so you will have to ask to see it – normally a run-of-the-mill Victorian font is used for christenings. Near this Victorian font on the north wall is a panel showing the Royal Arms which is actually a piece of weaving also by Mary Whitbread. On the south wall note a set of commandment boards – very dark and dingy, but still decipherable.

Flamstead

➤ Along with Markyate, Flamstead is 'pushed' up into a little western corner of the county right against the Bedfordshire border but separated from Luton by the ever-present M1 motorway. A mile or so to the west of the village is Beechwood, now a private school, standing in grounds

Praying children on Saunder's tomb at St Leonard's church, Flamstead

landscaped by Capability Brown, which was built in 1702 close to the site of a Benedictine nunnery founded circa 1150, but Flamstead's chief glory lies in the church of St. Leonard.

The old guidebooks tended to concentrate on the memorials in the church especially that of Thomas Saunders at the end of the south aisle – a large altar tomb of black marble with figures of his deceased children on the top – but it is the wall paintings here which dominate. Pevsner writes 'apart from St. Albans, the most important series in the county'. They were only revealed between 1930 and 1932 with further revelations during restoration in 1974.

On the north wall of the north aisle there are remnants of The Betrayal, The Last Supper, The Crucifixion, The Mocking of Christ, The Entombment, The Crowning with Thorns and The Resurrection. Possibly, however, the clearest painting is above the chancel arch showing 'Christ in Glory' together with an outline of a building. Buy the little church guidebook, and then with care and imagination each picture will vividly materialise.

Just to the north of the church are the Saunders Almshouses, founded in 1669 by the gentleman of the church memorial.

Flaunden

Sir George Gilbert Scott, the architect responsible for St. Pancras Station, or more correctly the Midland Grand Hotel at St. Pancras, and the Albert Memorial, designed the church here in 1838 – it was his first. Although he seemed to belittle it later in his memoirs as 'the poor barn designed for my uncle', it was the start of a 44 year career during which he designed not only six churches in the county, but was also involved nationwide in the restoration of nearly 500 churches and 39 cathedrals.

The 'new' St. Mary Magdalene holds some antiquities because the 15th century font and some medieval tiles together with three bells (one dated 1578) were installed in Scott's church from the 'old' one, which was built circa 1230 right on the Bucks boundary.

There are one or two attractive cottages in this Chiltern outpost but it is not worth looking for the original church. Only a few crumbling walls remain in trees on the banks of the river Chess at Flaunden Bottom, nearer to Latimer (Bucks) than Flaunden.

Furneux Pelham

The name gives the clue to the antiquity of this quiet village – 850 years have passed since the Norman family of de Furneux gave the village part of its name (even though some guide books insist on 'Furneaux'). The Early English church dates from the middle of the 13th century although the embattled flint tower is a hundred years older circa 1370. The tower has the county feature of a leaded spike, but perhaps of greater interest is the detail surrounding the clock below a window of the bell chamber. Possibly of the 17th century, a figure of Father Time surmounts it proclaiming that 'Time Flies' and 'Mind Your Business', one inscription above the clock, and one below it.

The embattled south porch has two storeys with uneven windows, but it was mainly rebuilt in 1869 during the general Victorian church restoration – although this eventually resulted in Pre-Raphaelite memorial windows by William Morris and Edward Burne-Jones for the Calvert family.

A number of pargetted cottages in the village and the attractive Star hostelry with its ceiling hung with bygones and supplied with beer by a very local brewery are dominated by the Hall with some 16th century stepped gables and some 17th century alterations on the west side which gave them a curved shape. This manor house is not open to the public although the rose gardens are on special occasions.

Gilston

➤ In the middle of double-bended Pye Corner on the A414, a road leads off to the church and Gilston Park, so in effect Gilston is split into two parts – the clutch of houses and cottages round the 17th century The Plume of Feathers Inn or just off the main road with church and Gilston Park more than a mile away.

The neo-Tudor mansion of Gilston Park, now the research centre of a pharmaceutical firm, stands near the site of the former New Place, successively the home of the Chauncys, the Gores and after 1701, the Plumers. William Plumer was the last of the line, and after he died in 1822, his other mansion described in one of Lamb's *Essays of Elia* was demolished (see Widford) in the following year and New Place disappeared to be replaced by Gilston Park in 1852.

The Royal Commission Inventory of Historical Monuments actually has a photograph of the late 13th century screen but I have to take Pevsner's word for it that it is 'a survival of first-rate importance' because here, once again, the church was locked with no indication as to where one could lay one's hands on the key.

Graveley

➤ An old milestone at the south end of the village opposite 'Mushroom Cottage' lets you know that you are 33 miles from London but this was put up when Graveley was astride the Great North Road. This explains the old coaching inns of the 18th century, The George and Dragon and The Rose and Crown, but now the A1(M) has taken a lot of the traffic, although the old road makes a quick 'rat run' from Baldock into parts of Stevenage.

Up a little lane by the Citroen garage is St. Mary's church, standing right next to 17th century Graveley Hall Farm. The embattled church tower of circa 1480 has a spike, but unusually, this is in the form of a cross. The usual Victorian restoration took place in 1887 but one of the bells in the bell-chamber is dated 1589. In the churchyard there is not only a graveboard, or 'bedhead memorial', but also a grave cover to foil the body-snatchers.

Due east up a little lane opposite the church entrance but a mile further on, the ruined St. Etheldreda stands surrounded by a wire fence in a field next to 17th century Chesfield Manor Farm. Last used in 1731 it is still a place of pilgrimage.

Great Amwell

The church of St. John the Baptist is of interest because of its apse, one of only three in the county, but it is the romantic water-garden with its monuments which is important here. Between 1609 and 1613 Sir Hugh Myddleton completed the herculean task of cutting what became known as the New river, from the sources of nearby wells in Great Amwell through to Clerkenwell in London, to provide the capital with a better water supply.

Some 200 years later Robert Mylne, an architect and an engineer on the New river, created the water garden below the church and on two islands, and erected typically 17th century urn-like monuments. The larger monument carries a tribute to Sir Hugh whilst the smaller monument carries a poem:

> Amwell, perpetual be thy stream
> Nor, e'er thy springs be less
> Which thousands drink who never dream
> Whence flows the boon they bless
>
> Too often thus ungrateful man
> Blind and unconscious lives,
> Enjoys kind Heaven's indulgent plan
> Nor thinks of him who gives.

These lines were by Archbishop Nares, a friend of Mylne, but often attributed to John Scott who did, in 1776, write a poem called *Amwell, a Prospect of Ware and the County adjacent*, but it was about the village itself. He is more famous for his grotto which, happily, still exists (see Ware).

The Norman church with its apse dates from the 11th century although the tower and west door are circa 1420. The chancel arch is as old as the chancel – the end of the 11th century – and unusually on either side is a a very large hagioscope or squint but of an unknown date. The only other point of interest is the pulpit dating from the beginning of the 17th century, supposedly brought from the Archiepiscopal Palace in Croydon, and adorned with six Termini Caryatids or female heads made, it is said from the old sounding board of the pulpit in St. Paul's in 1696 – a complicated history indeed!

There are many interesting memorials in the churchyard including one built by Robert Mylne for himself and his family and the remains of the stocks stand near the gate, although in a very poor state.

Great Gaddesden

➤ The river Gade is the visually dominating feature here, it metaphorically links the scattered parts of the parish together. Approach the area from Gaddesden Row where there are remains of medieval fishponds and a tumulus of unknown origin, but these in the private grounds of Golden Parsonage. In the same area a fine collection of Stone Age flints and hunting tools (now in the British Museum) have been found. The road drops steeply down to the valley of the river past the entrance to Gaddesden Place, the home of the Halseys.

It was built for the Halsey family between 1768 and 1773 by James Wyatt – later very much involved with Ashridge – and after a disastrous fire in 1905, was rebuilt and now still proudly overlooks the valley. It is mentioned here, not because it is open to view, but because there are many memorials to the Halsey family in the church of St. John the Baptist on the other side of the river, in the middle of the village.

The east wall of the chancel is as early as the 12th century, but there are Roman bricks in its buttresses and some of the corner stones, clearly visible as you approach the church. A number of tomb chests in the churchyard stand immediately in front of this east wall but between the buttresses and under the east window there is a stone with 'IHS' cut into it twice – unfortunately there is also graffiti.

In the churchyard a grave cover and a bedhead graveboard also survive, but, in the church, there are over 20 monuments to the Halsey family in their chapel at the north-east end. There is also one on the north wall of the chancel to Thomas Halsey and his wife Frederica together with their four year old son, Ethelbert, who were drowned at sea.

There are commandment boards on either side of the altar, and angels on the roof corbels. These, however, are not old as may be read on a plaque recording that they were put up between 1912 and 1914, but possibly the most interesting feature here is the 15th century tower with a fine collection of gargoyles which vie with those at Willian. As at Willian, they are unrecorded by all except by Arthur Mee who writes that you will see 'no fiercer animal at Whipsnade than the gargoyles round the church tower'.

Back at the river and on the A4146 there is the attractive little hamlet of Water End and its old bridge – featured in many calendars over the years – and then, retracing one's tracks to where the road dropped down from Gaddesden Row, it can be seen that the Gade widens out into a pool between the two road bridges to make a photographer's paradise.

Great Wymondley

➤ A quiet village now between Willian and the larger Little Wymondley, Great Wymondley has, notwithstanding, a history which dates back to the Romans – a tessellated pavement was unearthed in a Roman dwelling house near Purwell Mill in 1884 – and possibly even as far back as the Stone Age, because prehistoric implements have also been found. Enclosed between the two roads to Little Wymondley, and south of the church, is an enclosure of the motte and bailey type where a Norman lord of the manor built his castle in what was originally a Roman settlement.

It could have been the same Norman who built St. Mary's church, whose chancel and nave contain a few Roman tiles found locally when it was erected in the 12th century. The chancel is one of only three in the county with an apse. In 1883 the building was much restored but it still has it south doorway of circa 1120 with a tympanum, the apsidal chancel and its 15th century nave roof still supported by corbels with heads on, or as Arthur Mee puts it, 'a medieval portrait gallery in stone – scowling barons, a king, a patient nun and women in curious square headdresses, a shaggy lion among them resembling the beasts on the 15th century tower'.

At the crossroads in the village is The Green Man and nearby the manor house. South of the church, past the restored Hornbeam Cottages, is Delamere House built circa 1600 on the site of a former building once occupied by Cardinal Wolsey.

Great Wymondley's tally of historical events was added to in June 1982 when, after opening the Chapter House in St. Albans Cathedral, Queen Elizabeth II came to the village to present The Best Kept Village plaque for that year.

Green

No, there is not one single village of that name but Birch Green, Cole Green, Eastend Green, Letty Green and Staines Green are all situated within a rough rectangle of not much more than four square miles between the A414 and B158 with Hertingfordbury in the top-eastern corner. They all have an ancient pedigree and because they occupy space on the map, they should not be omitted.

They are all quiet villages with no special features, even the railway line was taken away by Dr. Beeching, so they are all truly 'hidden'. Back in 1903, the Little Guide had an entry for Cole Green: 'from the station little is to be seen except the Cowper's Arms and a few cottages'. On the other hand, the authoritative *Place-Names of Hertfordshire* traces them all back to the 13th century with Roxford Farm in Letty Green being in Domesday Book as Rochesforde.

There is a little church at Letty Green and across the A414, opposite the Green at Cole Green, are dilapidated lodges and gates – all that remains of the Cowpers' Panshanger Park.

Harpenden

The first and most obvious feature of the 'village', as it is known to all who live here despite the present population of 30,000 plus, is the existence of the common of some 238 acres. The common together with the greens in the High Street, Church Green and Leyton Green, with many trees still standing, makes Harpenden almost unique among small towns which, it must be admitted, it has now become. With industry confined to one small area and many hundreds commuting to London and elsewhere every day on the Bed-Pan line, Harpenden might appear to be just a dormitory town with, apparently, little to offer in the way of buildings or objects of architectural interest, but it is, in fact, around or near just those greens and the common, that this can be found to be quite erroneous.

As the common begins to narrow near the 'village' note the fine Town Sign, one of only three ornamental signs in the county, with its two shields naming Alzey in Germany and Cosne-Cours-sur-Loire in France which are Harpenden's 'Twin Towns', but immediately after, the architectural interest begins.

On the west side of the common and set back on either side of the Silver Cup public house, stand two historic houses in Leyton Road. One 'The Old House' (No 27) is basically a 16th century timber-framed building and was formerly The Bull Inn. The other is 'Coach Lane Cottage', at one time the home of Frank Salisbury, the artist.

On the east side, Harpenden Hall, the offices of the Town Council, is partly 16th century with 18th century additions but the main interest on the east side is the Moat House Hotel. This six-bayed building of circa 1700, previously the home of St. Dominic's Convent School, was successfully converted to its present state in 1971 without sacrificing any of its considerable architectural features, making it a fine counter-point to 'The Old House' back across the common.

This successful conversion of a listed building is reflected elsewhere in the town and particularly noticeable at Leyton Green. When a long-established and much missed family emporium (Anscombes) in Leyton Road was demolished to make way for the Waitrose Supermarket, Wellington House, the family home, was saved. Now, after virtually being rebuilt, although retaining its original exterior, it has become the offices of a Housing Association and adds lustre to Leyton Green.

Opposite the Glen Eagle Hotel and less noticeable than Wellington House because partly hidden behind a wall but no less prestigious, is the former home of the Lydekker family. This is Harpenden Lodge which has been restored and converted, along with former stables, into flats – to win the designers 3rd prize in a nation-wide competition run by the Royal Institution of Chartered Surveyors and *The Times* newspaper.

72

Much less noticeable, unfortunately, is Bowers House which is virtually hidden by a parade of shops built in front of it in 1936. It now has an 18th century facade but originally it dates from early 16th century: you can obtain a view of its roof from the car park on top of Sainsburys! Immediately north of the aforementioned parade of shops, is a group of 17th century houses (65–73 High Street) which have been carefully preserved as offices and shops, even though there has been the tasteful infilling of Tollgate House.

Until recently at Fallows Green there stood a house with theatrical connections but now there is only a small estate which is called Pigeon Wick. Ellen Terry abandoned her early stage career in despair and lived there from 1864 to 1870 with one Edward Godwin, by whom she had two children. She professed herself 'very happy . . . and when my children were born, I thought of the stage less than ever'. A chance meeting in Harpenden with Charles Reade in 1870, however, led to her return to the stage and so to become one of the greatest actresses of the last hundred years.

Across the road in Church Green, is St. Nicholas' church where there is a brass tablet to one of the best known of the Lydekkers, Richard Lydekker, naturalist and author, whose death in 1915 was an immense loss to the science of natural history. The main body of the church is only 1862 but the tower of plastered flint is dated 1470, itself replacing an earlier central tower which was destroyed by fire earlier in the 15th century. It has the traditional battlements and spike, but they are not the end of the antiquities because there is a font of circa 1200 and the oldest monument in the tower is dated 1642, a tribute to Robert Rudston who lived in Harpenden Hall.

There is a window in the north transept to the family of the founder of the Rothamsted Agricultural Research Centre, Sir John Bennett Lawes. The offices are seen when driving over the common but Sir John was born in Rothamsted Manor in 1814 and the great world-renowned centre grew out of his interest in science after he inherited the estate in 1835.

The Manor is now a hall of residence for students at the Research Centre but visits are arranged from time to time to see this interesting building, parts of which date from medieval times although basically early 17th century. There is no road through the Park but it is reached via picturesque Hatching Green with its 17th century White Horse Inn at the start of the B487 road to Redbourn.

A favourite walk for residents is in the other direction over the bridge by the ford at Batford up to the 16th century mansion of Mackery End. Nearby is the farmhouse where Charles Lamb used to stay as described in 'Mackery End in Hertfordshire' in his *Essays of Elia*.

Hatfield

➤ Hatfield, both Old and New, and Robert Cecil's Hatfield House are well covered by a variety of illustrated publications both private and from the Tourist Board so there is no need to repeat the history. But there are several points of interest which merit a place in this book, and so take the church of St. Etheldreda first because it stands just outside the grounds of the Old Palace at the top of Fore Street. Robert Cecil, the 1st Earl of Salisbury did not live to see the completion of his magnificent new house in 1612, and he is buried in the Salisbury Chapel, the north chapel of St. Etheldreda, and he has a most remarkable tomb commissioned by his son William: the effigy of the Earl in full state dress lies on a black marble slab supported by the four kneeling Cardinal Virtues – Temperance, Justice, Fortitude and Prudence – but beneath the effigy lies a skeleton on a rough straw mat!

For many generations there were no notable holders of the title but in Victoria's reign the 3rd Marquess was three times Prime Minister. He died in 1903 and although there is a marble monument to him in Westminster Abbey, he is buried in the churchyard here. In the Salisbury Chapel is a replica in bronze of the Westminster Abbey monument showing him lying on a tomb of black marble wearing his mantle of the Order of the Garter. At the gates of Hatfield House, opposite the station, there is a seated statue to this descendant of Robert Cecil, the last nobleman to be Prime Minister.

Another Prime Minister, Lord Melbourne, and his eccentric wife Lady Caroline Lamb, are also buried here in the Lamb Vault. The Lamb family owned Brocket Park at that time having bought the estate when the Brocket succession ended, and some earlier Brocket memorials are in the Ponsbourne Aisle of the church.

In complete contrast to all this splendour, at the bottom of Fore Street is the 17th century Eight Bells Inn which has been immortalised for ever as the alehouse in which Charles Dickens in *Oliver Twist* made his fictional villain Bill Sykes take refuge after his murder of Nancy.

The A1(M) now goes through a tunnel and above ground alongside is the former de Havilland Aircraft factory where the Mosquito during the war and later the Comet, the first ever commercial jet airliner was built – now where the highly successful quiet 146 is built by British Aerospace.

Do not miss, however, two architectural achievements in the New Town – the swimming pool of 1965 with its 'hyperbolic paraboloid' roof and St. John's church with its sweeping roof built 1961–2 in the Hilltop neighbourhood.

Hemel Hempstead

➤ The New Town like the other three in the county, is well documented and although there are one or two interesting items to claim our attention in the newly developed areas, it is the Old Town that provides most of what may be labelled 'hidden'.

The County Library Service's book *A Hertfordshire Record* states, 'No English buildings survive in Hertfordshire from before the 10th century', although Domesday Book has quite a long entry for Hamelamesede, so that the natural starting point must be St. Mary's church. This is arguably the finest church in the county, and although Ashwell with its glorious tower may dispute this, nobody will disagree with its claim to be the finest Norman church. A large cruciform building of flint rubble with some Roman bricks in use, the church was begun in circa 1140 and finished some 40 years later with, of course, additions over the centuries. No great monuments here but all the Norman architectural features remain to be seen as well as the contemporary clerestory which is rare. There are old doorways in both the north and south porches but the crowning glory is the tall central tower with its big leaded spire rising to nearly 200 feet.

Overlooking the church in the High Street is the Old Town Hall erected in 1851 as Town Hall and Corn Exchange. After a Town Hall was built in the Marlowes in the New Town, this old building was threatened with demolition but it has been preserved for posterity. On the south side of the church is a walled garden which is entered by the Charter Tower – this is all that remains of a building which was pulled down to make way for the present Bury House nearby which dates from 1790. The tower owes its name to the tradition that Henry VIII presented a charter to the town in 1539 from the very window of this surviving porchway but the Royal Commission dates the tower as *late* 16th century. Tradition dies hard, however!

Back in the High Street, note the iron balcony railing of The Old Bell whilst at the beginning of George Street, there is a wooden balcony belonging to the 17th century King's Arms still overlooking what used to be a courtyard. All along the High Street are buildings which have survived at least two centuries, and if you look up, dates can be seen on the rainwater heads above the drain pipes – 1725, 1726, 1728 and 1730 are some of those visible. At the end of the High Street, overlooked by Nos 98/100 with its pargetting decoration, there is a cast-iron hand pump (which also incorporates a lamp) built by a local craftsman, John Cranstone. It carries the inscription 'Erected by public subscription 1848 J. Cross, Bailiff'. To the west of the church is Gadebridge Park formerly the grounds of the mansion of the Paston Cooper family, and there is a very attractive iron footbridge over the river Gade, also built by Cranstone a few years earlier in 1840.

Sir Astley Paston Cooper who lived in Gadebridge Park was sergeant-surgeon, not only to George IV and William IV, but also to Queen Victoria until he died in 1841. In a church with few great monuments, the monument to him is the most conspicuous. It has been written that Cooper 'elevated surgery, the operations of which before his time had been described as a series of frightful alternatives or hazardous compromises, into a science'.

Hertford

◄ Long before Hertforde featured in Domesday Book, the first National Synod, which was called by Theodore of Tarsus, was held in Hertford in A.D. 673, to which came the five Bishops of the ancient Kingdoms. There were celebrations in the town in 1973 to honour the 13th centenary of this event, and a sculpture and plaque recording this can be seen on the wall of the Castle Hall off Millbridge. Where the Synod met may only have been a convenient spot with hardly a settlement but 200 or so years later King Alfred defeated the Danes, and soon after the Conquest the Normans built the castle within the Saxon stronghold put up after the Danes were vanquished.

The castle today is, in reality, the gatehouse of 1461 built between the original outer and inner bailey and is all that remains of the original castle. It is now part of the Council Offices, and is open on the first Sunday in the months May to September for guided tours: the gardens, however, are open to all daily.

In Fore Street there is as fine a display of pargetting as can be seen anywhere, all along Nos 3–11 and opposite on the Salisbury Arms. There is more pargetting on Weir Cottage

Hertford Castle

facing the car park off St. Andrew's Street – well worth seeing even if you have to leave your car somewhere!

In Railway Street, the Friends Meeting House of 1670 is said to be the oldest Meeting House which was purpose-built and still in use. Back in Fore Street is the Shire Hall of 1768–9 built by Robert Adam's brother, James, and nearby is the 1857 Corn Exchange. Further on, another purpose-built building, the Christ's Hospital School for Girls, has been transformed into 'prestigious' offices. The girls went to join the boys in Horsham in 1985 after nearly 300 years of Bluecoat occupation but note the little 1721 Bluecoat statues on the gates and in niches on the side of the original 1778 girls school.

The dual carriageway through the town is a mixed blessing but it does allow much freer access to view all the historic buildings in the centre. Get a guidebook and take time to view – it can be very rewarding.

Hertford Heath

➤ Little Amwell, formerly in the parish of All Saints, Hertford, became a separate parish in 1864 with Holy Trinity church erected in 1863, but now you will not find the name on the ordnance survey map – the district is now generally called Hertford Heath.

Apart from the fountain on the village green, there would not be a lot to report if it was not for what started as a training school for the East India Company in 1809 but is now the well-known public school, Haileybury College. After the East India Company closed down in 1857, the school started operating in 1862. The chapel with its gigantic dome by Sir Arthur Blomfield in 1876 is conspicuous for miles around, but the original buildings were by William Wilkens, the architect of Downing College, Cambridge and University College, London.

Hertingfordbury

➤ Until the A414 was diverted onto a bypass, Hertingfordbury was a very dangerous little village, albeit still very picturesque. Now it is comparatively tranquil again with car drivers gaining a better view of the Mimram Valley.

The White Horse dates from the 16th century, and now owned by Trust House Forte, is a popular hostelry and week-end conference centre. The church was founded in the 13th century but it virtually dates from 1850–3 when it was rebuilt by Earl Cowper, one of many Cowpers who were lords of the manor at nearby Panshanger Park. The estate was landscaped by Humphrey Repton, but the house has vanished, demolished in 1954 but leaving what is supposed to be the oldest oak tree in England – The Great Oak of Panshanger.

In the churchyard there is a sarcophagus to Sarah Lady Cowper who died in 1719, whilst inside there are memorials to other Cowpers as well as a standing wall-monument with recumbent effigy of Lady Calvert, who was the mother of Lord Baltimore, the founder of the colony at Maryland, in 1634. Note also the benches carved by Joseph Mayer of Oberammergau in 1875.

Hexton

➤ The church of St. Faith is not all that it appears to be when viewed from the Hitchin-Barton road. Externally having a 19th century look, internally it is basically 13th century, with a double-decker pulpit, a manorial pew (complete with fireplace), commandment boards and some interesting tablets.

Outside again, you will see that the 15th century tower has its own singular peculiarity: the back of it looks like a film set because two sides collapsed in 1947 leaving the bells, still in position, exposed for all to see! The bells were rehung in 1959 by a member of the de Latour family, not in the ruined tower but at ground level below the west window. Unfortunately you are unable to see them because they have been walled up.

The de Latour family, remembered on some of the church tablets, escaped from France during the French Revolution and it was Joseph Andrew de Latour who, after settling in the village as an English Squire, not only rebuilt the church but helped to keep the village prosperous. His wife Caroline, who outlived him by a score of years, put up the pump at the crossroads in 1846. Although no longer in use, the attractive pump serves two new purposes: it supports a wrought-iron street lamp and also two signposts.

The Ordnance Map shows that 'Ravensburgh Castle' lies in the Barton Hills just south of the village but this is, in fact, an Iron Age hillfort. No masonry here, of course, but keen archaeologists after tackling the walk in the hills to reach what The Royal Commission calls 'the best specimen of a Pre-Roman Camp in the county', may like to refresh themselves back in the village at The Raven with its intriguing sign 'The Raven of Ravensburgh'.

High Cross

◄ Up the hill from Wadesmill and the river Rib, Ermine Street (A10) passes through High Cross in a flash but, apart from the early Victorian church of St. John with its stained glass by Selwyn Image, a disciple of Burne-Jones, the interest lies on the fringes of this miniscule hamlet.

Up the first turning left going north on a field at a spot shown on the OS map as Standon Green End (often confusingly linked with the village of Standon in many guidebooks) is a memorial stone which records where the very earliest flight of any kind over British soil ended, in a hot air balloon by Vincent Lunardi on 15th September, 1784. On top of the stone is a plate with engravings of a balloon and a compass together with a lengthy description which begins—

> 'Let Posterity know
> and knowing be astonished
> that
> on the 15th day of September 1784
> Vincent Lunardi of Lucca in Tuscany
> The First Aerial traveller in Britain. . . .'

and so on.

In the other direction back down the hill towards Wadesmill is a small obelisk by the roadside which records 'on the spot where stands this monument in the month of June 1785 Thomas Clarkson resolved to devote his life to bringing about the abolition of the Slave Trade'.

Wilberforce is the name which usually comes to mind when discussing the abolition of slavery but it was Clarkson who did most of the spadework. *The Dictionary of National Biography* says 'It is almost impossible to over-rate the effect of his unceasing perseverance'.

Hinxworth

➤ A glance at the map will reveal that Hinxworth is the most northerly of the county's villages – a few hundred yards or so to the north-west and you are in Bedfordshire – but the chief attraction here is a short way in the other direction as you approach the village off the A1 from Baldock.

Hinxworth Place once the home of one of the county's historians, Robert Clutterbuck, is the best preserved stone building in the county, the remains of a larger house built in the 15th century. Long before Clutterbuck, it was once inhabited by some Cistercian monks of the Monastery of Pipewell in Northants and it is supposed to be haunted. Ghostly processions of monks have been seen to come through a wall, apparently on their way to or from worship through a doorway long ago bricked up!

Back in the little village a village clock on top of a tower is the war memorial and the church of St. Nicholas is an odd mixture of styles of a number of centuries. The nave and the west tower, both embattled, are of the 15th century but the chancel, looking as if it had been added as an after-thought, is of brick having been rebuilt in the 18th century.

Hitchin

➤ Arthur Mee, in 1939, wrote thus about Hitchin: 'It is old-world England wherever we turn in this small town . . . the streets are attractive with old houses, some so low that we may touch the eaves from the pavements. . . .'

A guidebook will come in handy when tracing not only the well established but also the new developments so a few points to what may be hidden in this ancient town will be useful.

It is the church and its attractive setting by the river Hiz which is the visual centre, although it is not improved by the car park, previously the site of the Tuesday Market, to the east of it.

Tilehouse Street and Bridge Street together are the two most architecturally interesting streets with houses of the 15th century onwards, but unfortunately not helped by the Job Centre and the huge Insurance Offices in Old Carlton Road. Look out for the little crane above a piano shop, opposite to the entrance to The Priory which was a mansion put up in 1770–7, but incorporating fragments of the cloisters of the Carmelite Priory founded early in the 14th century and destroyed at the Dissolution. Ironically it is the same insurance company which is now the owner of the Priory – it has been saved for the town but will be the boardroom for the company. At the top of Tilehouse Street, now blocked off, is the Coopers Arms which is said to have been the Tylers Guildhall and dating from the 15th century.

Also in Tilehouse Street is a Baptist Chapel – the present building is 1844 although restored in 1894 – where they have a chair given to them by John Bunyan who used to preach on the site in the 1660s.

From Baptists to Quakers – a modernistic building on the corner of Bedford Road and Paynes Park is, in fact, the Friends Meeting House erected in 1958. Brand Street, the continuation of Bedford Road towards Bancroft, offers two Town Halls, one of 1840 and one of 1901 but many will find more fun in the fascinating mural depicting the town's history on the outside wall of Sainsburys!

In Bucklersbury, Sun Street and Bancroft a number of old buildings do manage to survive the developers, as does the Skynners Almshouses in Bancroft dated 1670 and 1698, but the chief glory of Hitchin is St. Mary's church with its massive tower on what must be one of the most attractive ecclesiastical sites in the county. It is worth buying the short history of the church by the celebrated Hitchin historian, the late Reginald Hine, because there are so many treasures here, but note the two storeyed porch with the two sided sundial above it, the 15th century screen with carved angels on the south chapel which has angels in the roof, a pulpit of circa 1500 and a twelve sided font ornamented with defaced figures of saints.

Hoddesdon

◄ The former hamlet of Hoddesdon is now much larger than the originally larger Broxbourne and had, in fact, its own market by the 13th century. The market today is held all round the somewhat clumsy-looking clock tower of 1835 which stands on the site of a chapel with the 16th century bell of the chapel contained within it. Many of such towers have been swept away because of modern road conditions but this one remains despite the odd traffic arrangements here, and it also provides a counterpoint to the disastrous tower block which dominates the town. This block remains when many antiquities like The Bull and The Old Market house have been swept away, but that is progress. The Golden Lion, The Swan and The Bell still remain as does also Rawdon House of 1622, offices now since 1975, but at the turn of the century it was a nunnery.

There is no church of note here, only a Victorian one of 1864 with its red brick tower and a pyramidal roof of 1888, so on to Hoddesdon's one great treasure which stands between the New river (and just over the railway) and the river Lea – the preserved 1443 gateway of Rye House, the earliest building of brick in the county.

Rye House, once the resting place of The Great Bed of Ware, is now a feature of the Lea Valley Regional Park but in 1683 was the key factor in what became known as The Rye House Plot. The plot, engineered by some ex-Cromwellian Republicans and other malcontents, was to assassinate Charles II and his brother James, the then Duke of York. The plotters apparently knew that the King's party would take a route which led past Rye House whilst returning from a stay in Newmarket so they planned to block the road with carts, and then the deed would be carried out. The course of history was not changed because a fire at the house occupied by the King and his brother forced them to leave Newmarket a day or two earlier than they had intended. They thus escaped assassination although the plot was, in any case, betrayed and most of the conspirators were executed.

Holwell

➤ Right up against the Bedfordshire border north of Hitchin, Holwell was transferred to Hertfordshire in 1897 and, at first glance, does not, as one writer puts it, look as if it had any history prior to the 19th century. Wrong, because it had its place in Domesday Book but no sign now of the two mills of the Inventory. Perhaps the oldest relic is the homestead mill on the Pirton Road.

The present St. Peter's church was built 1877–9 on the site of and using much material from an older church, including a 15th century door in the north wall of the nave. From the old church there is an interesting 1515 brass to Richard Wodehouse, presumably a former rector, with, instead of heraldry, two 'Wodehouses' or wild men which made a little pun on his name.

Hormead, Great & Little

➤ Originally one village in the possession of Count Eustace at the time of Domesday, it was divided soon after 1100 when the names of Hormead Magna and Hormead Parva came into use.

Little Hormead, now virtually just a straggling hamlet to the south of its 'greater' companion, on the road between Furneux Pelham and the B1368 has one precious treasure preserved in its lovely little Norman church of St. Mary. If you can find the keeper of the key of this normally locked church with its nave of circa 1140, but no heating or lighting, you will be rewarded by seeing what Pevsner calls 'the most lavish display of 12th century ironwork' on the Norman north door. There is a prettily decorated font of circa 1310 and the south door is also Norman, although the little brick porch was added in the 18th century.

Great Hormead, not too long ago, was known for the remains of two windmills in a county which can boast very few of these survivors of a bygone age, but sadly they are no more although you may find a few relics in the bushes. Now, the village is known for its charming timber-framed thatched cottages and, although very difficult today, for its quiet separation from the main roads of the county.

In a field down a lane off the road to Brent Pelham is an early 16th century manor house with stepped gables and mullioned windows. The house was named 'The Brick House' when brick was only just becoming more generally used. Back in the village above the main street the church of St. Nicholas dates back to the late 13th century with a 15th century embattled tower. Like so many, the church was much renewed in 1872–3 but it still retains its Norman font and there is a memorial to local Lt. Col. Stables who was killed in 1815 at Waterloo – a grecian sarcophagus with the word 'Waterloo' on it in an oval laurel wreath.

Hunsdon

Hunsdon House figures much in Tudor times. Originally built in the middle of the 15th century, Henry VIII had it rebuilt in 1525, and not only did he and the Court stay there during outbreaks of the plague but all three of his children resided there at some time. Today it has dropped out of history and after much rebuilding in 1804, it is not open to the public, so switch your attention to St. Dunstan's church with its wooden porch, the oldest in the county and in position long before Henry VIII ever came to Hunsdon.

Inside despite the usual Victorian restoration, some treasures still remain: a Jacobean pulpit with a tester is backed up by what is considered to be the church's most handsome possession – a Jacobean screen in front of the Carey Chapel with its high family pews. The spike is alleged to have come from St. Albans Abbey.

Church and House are a little distance from the village, and when you go to look at the village itself, do not miss the octagonal dovecote now converted into a dwelling complete with chimney: not mentioned however, in Pevsner!

The village, which during the war was practically engulfed by an airfield from which Mosquito planes flew (see Salisbury Hall and London Colney), is unlike any other village in the county. It is distinctly 'Essex' in its appearance but nevertheless delightful, and everyone seems to make the extra effort with quantities of white paint to keep it so. An old pump, surrounded by railings, stands in the middle of the road in front of the ancient pumphouse, and there is a little village green. It is, however, the weatherboarding and the half-timbering which make the overall picture so attractive, and do not fail to inspect the village hall in the centre of the village opposite the green – they are very proud of their half-timbered hall here. Adjacent to the hall, however, is a most unusual feature on a cottage – two large carvings of horses acting like corbels beneath the overhang of the upper storey.

Ickleford

◆ Although originally cut off from Hitchin by the river Oughton, Ickleford inevitably has been overrun by Big Brother, but it is still very much a village as witnessed by the fact that it won the accolade of being the Best Kept Village in the county in 1983 and 1985.

The Old George is half-timbered and some of it dates back to the 16th century, but it is so overshadowed by modern housing that it is to the church that we turn to seek for the hidden Ickleford.

St Katherine's, sheltering among cedar trees, was very largely restored in 1859 by Sir George Gilbert Scott, who also added a south aisle and a south chapel. On the other hand the nave is circa 1150, both south doorway and the now blocked north doorway are 12th century with true Norman zigzag arches and the nave's 15th century roof is supported by grotesque stone corbels.

As you leave the church, you will see that the south porch, unlike the tower, is embattled with a little niche centrally over the doorway, and you should search in the churchyard for the grave of one Henry Boswell, a local gypsy king who died during the reign of George III in 1780.

Kelshall

Kelshall, a one-time remote village on the northern edge of the county, can boast not one but two remains of medieval crosses. One, the base of a village cross, stands in the middle of a small triangular green at a road junction near the church. Probably of the 14th century, it was found in 1906 and is now under the care of the County Council.

The other cross, probably of the next century, stands in the churchyard and has had a sundial added to it.

St. Faith's church, complete with embattled tower and spike, dates from the late 14th century and it has a two storey south porch with the upper storey approached by a stair turret. The door of the south porch is original and its old lock and key are preserved. A curiosity is a wall recess 12 feet high and under 2 feet wide in the north aisle. The purpose of this has never been properly understood but it was probably used for the safe keeping of banner-staves, crosses and other pre-Reformation ornaments.

Kimpton

▬► The White Horse Inn, although much restored, is of the 17th century, but the church is supreme here both in age, architecture and because it overlooks a village which appears in Domesday Book and was known to the Saxons as Kimeton.

The nave is dated as early as the 12th century with aisles added circa 1200. The two storeyed porch and the embattled tower plus spike were added in the 15th century which strangely makes them still not as old as the oldest bell here of mid-14th century.

There are two medieval screens and some poppyhead benches, also traces of paintings of angels to note under lancet windows in the chancel, but these hardly class as important in any real study of church wall paintings.

Memorials to the Brand family who became Lords Dacre and later Viscounts Hampden abound, and this guides us to a real piece of hidden Hertfordshire. The family lived at Kimpton Hoo, a 17th century mansion in grounds laid out by 'Capability' Brown with various buildings by Sir William Chambers (who designed the Pagoda in Kew Gardens) and still marked on the OS map. The house was demolished in 1958, the follies are gone but a bridge survives which can be found on a track off the Codicote to Whitwell road.

Kings Langley

▬► The village got its name because of the Royal Palace, built by Henry III at what was then called 'Langley', and the only connection today with 'Royal' Langley is forever recorded in the play *Richard II* by our greatest dramatist. Richard II did not use Berkhamsted because he preferred Langley. During his last fateful absence, the Queen remained and Shakespeare sets Act III scene 4 in the garden of the Palace in 1399. Here the Queen learns from the gardener of her husband's overthrow by Bolingbroke, the future Henry IV, and she then exclaims:

'Gardener, for telling me this
news of woe
I would, the plants thou
graft's may never grow'.

That prayer has been more than fulfilled, as garden, Palace and all are gone with just a few stones remaining. This, of course, did not happen all at once but a final fragment, a wine cellar of 1292 excavated when foundations were being dug for new buildings of the Rudolph Steiner School on the site of the Palace at the top of Langley Hill, was recorded, photographed, then sadly filled in and covered by a new gymnasium in 1970. What is visible, however, are the remains of a Dominican friary which was established in 1312, where the body of Edmund of Langley, who was born in the Palace in 1341, was interred until it was removed to the parish church after the Dissolution. The Old Palace Inn opposite the gates of the Rudolph Steiner School, and the place-name itself, are now the only reminders of these medieval events on the top of Langley Hill.

Back on the main road, the road viaduct of the M25 over canal and railway is a fine piece of architectural engineering which this place may become proud of, but people of Kings Langley have perhaps more reason to be proud of the great paper mills which provide many with work.

On a much more modest scale, take a look at the 'pretty' iron veranda on The Rose and Crown Inn before going down Church Lane opposite and into All Saints church. Here is the fine tomb of Edmund of Langley, who was the 5th son of Edward III and was also the very first Duke of York. The tomb is surrounded by alabaster heraldry and is, apparently, very similar to that of his eldest brother, the Black Prince, in Canterbury Cathedral. The Black Prince was the father of the unfortunate Richard II.

The reredos, crammed with figures, is comparatively modern (1878) but the Jacobean pulpit complete with carvings of cockerels and a tester is a perfect little gem.

Kings Walden

➤ A manor house here, lasting from Elizabethan times until 1889, when it was demolished and a new one built, was replaced yet again in 1972.

Although the gardens are, on occasions, open to the public the Bury is not, so no need to linger but a sight of it can be glimpsed from the churchyard.

A 14th century screen, painted on both sides, has ogee-arched tracery and is of the same date as the west tower which is embattled and has a thin spike but is rather messy looking!

The village virtually splits into two hamlets with Parsonage Farm being midway between the two. In the southern half there are some 19th century gabled cottages, some half-timbered, whilst to the north there is the little shop and post office. An unusual curiosity here or rather two. On the side of the post office is the only Edward VII wall letter box in the county, whilst opposite the church entrance is one of only two George V wall boxes, the other being in Little Gaddesden.

Knebworth

➤ A southern outpost of Stevenage, Knebworth, like Gaul, is divided into two parts – the old and the new. The new grew up around the station and before the A1(M) was opened, was always busy with through road traffic to the north. There is nothing that could not have stayed hidden if it was not for St. Martin's church of 1914, one of Sir Edwin

Lutyens most remarkable churches. He designed a number of buildings in Knebworth including the golf clubhouse (1908) but the church is the most interesting with its excessively far-projecting roof eaves. Difficult to describe viv-a-vis traditional churches – see it for yourself and make up your own mind. He did not even finish the job, it was completed by Sir Albert Richardson in 1963–4 with a cupola at the west end.

Old Knebworth, however, is completely different and does, in fact, have a history before Domesday Book, in which it is listed as Chenepeworde. It runs along the eastern edge of the Park and is literally one of the smallest villages of the county with almshouses and picturesque lodge gates into the Park.

The original parish church of St. Mary and St. Thomas is in the Park, and attractive because of its position but otherwise uninteresting architecturally as far as the exterior is concerned, except for the 15th century tower with its gargoyles. Inside it is a different matter with a wealth of Lytton memorials, many in the baroque style. Note also two tombstones of 1938 and 1940 by Lutyens to two nannies of the family in the churchyard. Inside again, there is a complete set of 15th century benches in the nave, an octagonal font of circa 1480 and a pulpit of the 18th century but with carved panels of Flemish origin, one of them dated 1567.

Little need be said about the Park and its activities, all fully documented in guidebooks etc. Knebworth House as seen today is the romantic conception of Sir Edward Bulwer-Lytton who embellished the red brick of the original Tudor house in the middle of the 19th century with all kinds of Gothic decoration. The Lytton family first came to Knebworth in 1490 and it is still the family home. The house is open at stated times and the Hon. David Lytton Cobold welcomes 'all our visitors – strangers and old friends alike'!

Lemsford

➤ Long before the present A1 motorway allowed the horseless carriage to thunder along unimpeded by irritants like narrow village lanes, Lemsford was on the stage coach route to the North, and, despite its proximity to Welwyn Garden City, still retains its 'olde worlde' village appearance. In the centre of the village, one of the county's many water-mills – reputedly the one referred to in the old ballad of *Nellie Dean* – has been converted into offices but as a Department of Environment Grade II listed building, the exterior remains intact albeit with a new look.

Virtually rebuilt in 1986, the curiously named Long Arm and Short Arm pub stands alongside the old coach route, but by including the tiny hamlet of Cromer Hyde with Lemsford a contrast is The Crooked Chimney, once called Hornbeam Hall. It was originally The Chequers but as it was so widely known by its distinguishing feature it was renamed in 1968 – correctly labelled at last!

St. John's church was only built in the middle of the last century but on top of the tower as in medieval times long ago, dragon gargoyles channel rain down their water spouts.

Above all, however, it is Brocket Park which occupies a commanding position in Lemsford with grounds laid out by 'Capability' Brown, and stories about the eccentric Lady Caroline Lamb who scandalized society because of her tempestuous love affair with Lord Byron. The Hall is not open to the public and, as it has now become a luxury hotel and Conference Centre, has no place here. On the other hand there are footpath rights of way through the park so Brown's lake created by widening the river Lea, and the Hall can both be admired from the splendid bridge of 1772 over the river after going through the screen of the pedimented lodges.

Letchworth

By coincidence my Little Guide to Hertfordshire was published in the same year that Ebenezer Howard began his great experiment – on 1st September 1903 the First Garden City Ltd. was registered with an authorised capital of £300,000, and on the 9th October there was a formal opening of the First Garden City with Earl Grey presiding.

The story of Howard's dream of 'a deliberately planned, self-contained town where the rural and the urban, beauty and utility, health, material comfort and productive industry should all find encouragement and expression' (Branch Johnson) has been well documented and there are many books available giving the complete history as well as biographies of Howard himself. So what remains 'hidden'?

The original plan incorporated the villages of Norton, Willian and Letchworth from which it took its name – the Little Guide refers to Leceworde in Domesday Book being the property of Robert Gernon, a Norman warrior who fought at Hastings and who is remembered in a road name. Willian is dealt with elsewhere, Norton has St. Nicholas' church with an early 13th century font, a 17th century pulpit with a canopy and some 15th century benches, but linger awhile in what was the old village of Letchworth. The Post Office, because of its age, gets a place in the Royal Commission's Inventory and it is still there despite being on the A505 main road from Hitchin to Baldock. 'In the middle of the village' (the Royal Commission took no notice of the great social upheaval in the First Garden City!) is how it is described and 'probably of the 17th century'. The little church of St. Mary has a nave of the 12th century, and a chancel of the 13th. Its little bell-cote was added in the 16th century. On a north-east window sill in the nave, there is a stone effigy of a knight, only two feet long, who is holding his heart in his hands. This is dated circa 1300 and the door in the south porch has 13th century iron hinges.

Letchworth Hall, built in 1620, at one time the home of the eccentric parson the Revd. John Alington, is now a hotel.

This is matched by The Cloisters in Barrington Road in this same area, as Pevsner puts it 'a romantic composition' erected in 1907 by someone who many also would have called eccentric, Miss Annie Lawrence, a wealthy spinster, whose only aim was to further the study of callisthenics, philosophy and moral improvement. It now is part of next-door St. Christopher's school.

Leverstock Green (& Pimlico)

The WI claim that Leverstock Green still retains a strong village atmosphere despite the fact that it is now just one of the constituent parts of Hemel Hempstead, and it surely deserves a place here anyway because of the marvellous topiary animals (cat, dog and peacock) at Rose Cottage to be seen as you arrive on the St. Albans Road.

Maybe just a neighbourhood of the New Town now, but among other old farmhouses Westwick Row Farm is part of a cruck-framed hall-house, rebuilt in the 16th century. The little flint church of 1849 with its double bell-cote, looks out over a large village green near to where the Abbots Langley road meets up with the St. Albans Road, and the original school of 1840, known as Old School House, still exists in the Abbots Langley/Bedmond Road. Down that road, between the village and Bedmond, the birthplace of Nicholas Breakspear, is the little hamlet of Pimlico where a foursided clock sits, somewhat precariously, on top of a barn which has been restored.

Lilley

One of the two villages bypassed by the Luton to Hitchin bypass, so if you turn off by the lonely public house opposite Dog Kennel Farm you have breathing space to stop and enjoy the landscape without danger.

In St. Peter's church there are memorials to Thomas Docwra, who lived at Putteridge Bury just up the main-road
above Dog Kennel Farm, and there are rampant Docwra lion
crests on many of the cottage walls and gateposts.

One of the cottages is 17th century and when John Bunyan
was being persecuted, he ministered to his little flock in its
cellar and the hiding place is still in existence.

The church is only 1870–1 on the site of a medieval 12th
century one, but a few of the medieval bits remain plus a
15th century clunch font.

Little Berkhamsted

This 'Berkhamsted' has no connection with the town
of Berkhamsted in the west of the county, at one time called
'Great' to differentiate it, but like its namesake has a history
reaching at least as far back as Domesday Book.

At first glance there is nothing particularly exciting here
apart from a neat and well kept village but, of course,
nothing can hide the marvellous folly, now called Stratton's
Observatory. The traditional story is that retired Admiral
John Stratton built his tower so that he could observe the
shipping passing up and down the river Thames from the
top window. Even at 350 feet above sea level this would have
been an impossibility but he probably helped to solve an
unemployment problem!

In modern times, Brian Johnston, the well-known radio
cricket commentator was born here but we must go into the
church of St. Andrew to find out about the most famous local
son. The chancel altar was given in memory of Thomas Ken,
born in the parish in 1637, who grew up to become Chaplain
to Charles II and finally Bishop of Bath and Wells. He is best
remembered for his hymn *Glory to Thee, my God this night* and
the doxology *Praise God from whom all blessings flow*, and the
fact that he was one of the seven Bishops who refused to
read James II's Declaration of Indulgence in 1688.

Stratton's Observatory at Little Berkhamsted

In St. Andrews nothing but some monuments remain of the church built in 1647, it is mainly Victorian restoration work but note more stained glass of William Morris & Co of 1911 in the nave.

Little Gaddesden

➤ The very opposite to its 'Great' namesake, the larger Little Gaddesden is a long straggling village, with an almost equally long village green, stretching between the hamlets of Ringshall and Hudnall but, at all times, it is Ashridge and its Park which are omnipresent.

Coming into the village from Nettleden in the south-east, what strikes the eye first is an octagonal dovecote, at one time part of Home Farm, but now incorporated into a dwelling house. At the start of the green stands what appears to be a war memorial, but which is in fact a memorial to Adelaide, the beloved wife of the 3rd Earl of Brownlow. The panels state that she was 'Born 1844 Married 1868 Died 1917' and round the base can be read the legend 'Mercy and Truth have met together, Righteousness and Peace have kissed each other'.

Further down the green there is the real war memorial – war memorial panels added to the Lady Marian Alford Memorial, a most unusual piece of work which backs on to John of Gaddesden's House. This is a well restored and enlarged timber-framed house but undoubtedly of the 15th century with an overhanging upper floor. This present house, because it is of the 15th century, can only be a second building on the site, but keeping the name of the original one erected by John of Gaddesden himself. He died in 1361 after becoming the first Englishman to be made Court Physician to both King Edward II and King Edward III. If there is any confusion, it is not of importance as you look at the building. It is the exterior which concerns us not its history, so stand, stare and enjoy the fine pargetting to be seen on the over-hang.

A little further back towards the dovecote over a hedge behind the Lady Brownlow Memorial, the manor house of 1576 can be seen with its turrets and stepped gables.

Round the corner from John of Gaddesden's House, and standing quite on its own down a narrow road is St. Peter and St. Paul church which is, according to Pevsner, 'architecturally less important than for its monuments'. The south porch was rebuilt in 1830 by Sir Jeffry Wyatville whilst engaged on the rebuilding of Ashridge. There are 17th century carved poppyheads but it is the exceptionally full and varied series of monuments to the occupants of Ashridge, the Egerton family, the Earls and Dukes of Bridgewater, right on down to the 3rd and last Duke who died in 1803, the inspiration behind the Grand Union Canal which flows right through the county, which command attention.

The 3rd Duke of Bridgewater, who in theory was longer in ownership than anyone else, but hardly ever in residence, allowed Ashridge gradually to fall into complete disrepair. He was far too busy backing James Brindley's canal projects and earning himself the title of 'The Father of British Inland Navigation'. The Monument, by Sir Jeffry Wyatville, erected in 1832 in his honour – the Ashridge guidebook calls him 'The Canal Duke' – stands in the park in direct eye-catching line from the house. Although now somewhat obscured by trees, it does overlook Aldbury.

As for Ashridge itself, originally dating from 1283, and where Queen Elizabeth I was virtually a prisoner between 1553 and 1556, it is now a Management College. Books are available giving its full history and the beautiful gardens, in which both 'Capability' Brown and Humphrey Repton, his disciple, had a hand, are open to the public on Saturday and Sunday afternoons between April and October.

Little Hadham

➤ The village of Little Hadham, immediately north of its much larger neighbour, Much Hadham, was originally centred round what is now Church End where St. Cecilia's and a few cottages survive. At the beginning of the 16th century, the village began to group around where the Pelhams and Much Hadham road, roughly following the route of the river Ash, crossed Stane Street, which is today controlled by traffic lights – a necessary modern touch in a quiet village – with houses dated between 1672 and 1732.

The present village is virtually in three parts – Hadham Ford with two 17th century houses on Ford Hill and the war memorial, the centre with its clashing contrasts and Church End. At Church End also there is Hadham Hall, an Elizabethan mansion of circa 1575 – this is now a boarding school administered by the County Council but in danger of closing at the time of writing. In the grounds of the school complex is an early 17th century barn but the gatehouse, originally of an earlier building on the site, is older than the Hall. Just north of the Hall is a moated mound or tumulus but the smock mill so long, even in its ruinous state, a feature of the village, is no more, burnt down to its brick base in 1981.

St. Cecilia's, on the other hand, is still with us, with a nave possibly as old as the 12th century, although the church was dedicated to St. Edmund the Martyr before 1913.

Inside it is a little gem in that there are low box pews in front of a fine three-decker pulpit complete with its tester or sounding board, and it can be accurately dated 1633, the same date as the north transept and a gallery. There is a 15th century screen of an orthodox pattern but the church guide directs you to note the slab on the south side of the altar to Arthur Capel, who was 'murdered for his loyalty to his King'. The Capels lived in Hadham Hall and the King was Charles I.

Many consider that the wooden south porch is of more

100

interest than the fittings inside, a matter of opinion but it has survived remarkably well considering the timber work with trefoiled open panels and a cusped barge-board date from the early 15th century.

One final item of interest. In the churchyard is a tombstone to the memory of Captain William Harvey who died in 1807 at the age of 65. He accompanied Captain James Cook on his three voyages of discovery round the world.

Little Wymondley

◄ Great Wymondley has its earthworks but Little Wymondley can boast of something much more tangible – some very solid remains, uncovered during alterations in 1973, of the 13th century Augustinian priory which stands just north of the railway on the narrower of the two roads to Great Wymondley leading up from The Plume of Feathers. In fact, after the Dissolution, James Needham, Surveyor of the King's Works, built himself a house out of the priory remains, and the discoveries of 1973 add clerical ruins to what is now a farmhouse, and the original moat a series of ponds. However, there is still the medieval barn of 100 feet by 40 feet which must rival that at Croxley Green in its claim to be the second largest in the country.

The church of St. Mary is partly of the 15th century but much restored in 1875 as in so many places, with little of interest except to record that on the north wall of the chancel is a brass to James Needham of The Priory and his son. The inscription records that this was put up in 1605 by the grandson of one and the son of the other!

Just south of the church is late 16th century Wymondley Bury, complete with a moat and a dovecote – although when I inspected it last, it was in use as a coal store! One last word – The Plume of Feathers is 18th century, but The Buck's Head nearer to Hitchin is early 17th century.

London Colney

➤ Motorists speeding along the M25 motorway, whether in a clockwise or an anti-clockwise direction, cannot fail to notice what appears to be a monastic establishment between junctions 21A and 22, but it is passed in a flash and thoughts will then be on the next destination. It is, in fact, the All Saints Pastoral Centre which despite one's feelings about the motorway has been given greater exposure and attracts admiring glances.

The site, according to legend, was where St. Alban was captured, before his martyrdom on the spot where the cathedral stands, and so became a stopping place for pilgrims. The buildings did, indeed, start life as a convent in 1899, although the magnificent chapel, much admired by the late Sir John Betjeman, was only completed in 1964. When the nuns moved away to Oxford, the premises became a Catholic retreat centre.

Further along the road towards the village by Broad Colney bridge over the Colne is one of the London Coal Duty Boundary Markers, and another can be seen on what was, before the bypass was built, the main road near the seven arched bridge of 1772 – at one time attributed to Thomas Telford.

Although there are restored remnants of the inns dating back to coaching days, there is nothing to detain you further in London Colney, but do not leave the area before looking at Salisbury Hall, down a track off the old road from South Mimms and now virtually nestling under the lea of the M25 motorway. It is not, as it once was, open to the public but the romantic story of King Charles II and 'pretty, witty Nell Gwynne' will stay with the Hall even if it is converted into offices.

What is known as 'Nell Gwynne's Cottage' still stands by the moat, and here it was that the story began – a story denied and much doubted by the serious-minded concerning the eldest son of the King's mistress. I can do no better than repeat a learned paper quoted in the book *Picturesque*

Nell Gwynne's cottage at London Colney

Hertfordshire (1904) which asserts: 'Here, also, sweet Nell Gwynne of Old Drury came to recoup after the wear and tear of Court life. It was here that the wilful beauty held her infant child out of the window, and threatened to drop it in the placid water of the moat, being angry that he bore no title, and only withdrew it on the King exclaiming: "Nell, don't kill The Duke of St. Albans!"'.

Behind is the Mosquito Museum where the original Mosquito aeroplane prototype, designed at The Hall in the Second World War, can, with other de Havilland aircraft, be viewed on Sundays in the summer.

Long Marston

Long Marston has the reputation of being the village which witnessed the last witch tragedy, a terrible event which took place in 1751 and 16 years *after* the law against witchcraft had been repealed. Ruth and John Osborn, a harmless old couple and both over 70 years of age, were 'tried' by ducking in the so-called traditional way of testing for a witch – they would sink if innocent and float if guilty and so either way they were doomed! They both drowned, although poor John survived for a day or two, and one of the ringleaders, Thomas Colley, was hanged at Gubblecote Cross, just to the south of Long Marston. The hanging was boycotted by the majority of the locals because they felt that 'things had come to a pretty pass when a man was hanged for destroying a mischievous old witch!'.

Church ruins at Chesfield, Thundridge and Ayot St Lawrence are the normal antiquities of this kind which seem to attract attention in the guidebooks, but at the end of Chapel Lane in Long Marston the tower of the former 15th century church, demolished circa 1880, quietly moulders away by the half-timbered Old Church cottage. The new church of All Saints of 1882, which does not look very interesting from the outside, contains various fittings from the old church including an early 14th century window and a Norman arch on the north wall, together with the pulpit and screen inside.

Markyate

 Until 1880 Markyate, on old Watling Street, was partly in Hertfordshire and partly in Bedfordshire, but by 1957 the villagers could not have cared which county they were in – Watling Street had become the A5 and, on what was reputedly the busiest road in the county, lorries were doing dire damage to the old houses and cottages in the main street which, in places, was barely wide enough for two vehicles to pass.

In 1957 after the bypass was opened, with the M1 motorway opening not long afterwards, life became easier and the buildings were reprieved. In coaching days, Markyate was a staging post with a consequent great number of coaching inns and alehouses. Now there are only four with The Sun having a history at least back to 1605 and a plaque testifying that Dick Turpin did actually sleep there!

The bypass cut the little church of St. John the Baptist off from the village. It was, in fact, only built in 1734 in a corner of the grounds of Markyate Cell and it has nothing to comment on except a carved pulpit and a gallery, an unusual fitting in the county.

The Cell itself, which from a distance looks truly of Tudor construction was actually built circa 1825, on the site of a former 1539 mansion which was built after the dissolution of an old Benedictine nunnery started by Geoffrey de Gorham, 16th Abbot of St. Albans circa 1145. It is, of course, a private residence and not open to the public but is mentioned here because of the famous legend of The Wicked Lady, Lady Katherine Ferrers – supposedly a notorious highway-woman. She was mortally wounded in June 1660 on Nomansland at Wheathampstead whilst attacking a wagon but managed to get back home, but died on reaching safety (see Wheathampstead). The film of the same name, starring Margaret Lockwood and James Mason was inspired by the legend but it is a highly fictionalised account.

Meesden

By taking the longer route between Brent Pelham and Anstey, the village of Meesden appears, over the centuries, to have gradually slipped away from its little flint built church which has stubbornly stayed nearer the Essex border. It is only the lonely church that need keep you in this outpost of the county.

St. Mary's is basically 12th century but like many another church was rebuilt by the zealous Victorians in 1877. It is however, notable for two unusual features: a south porch built entirely of brick of circa 1530 and, in the chancel, a mosaic of glazed coloured tiles making various shapes in front of the altar. These are virtually unique in the county and the Royal Commission dates them as early 14th century.

Much Hadham

➤ If Benington and Westmill are the archetypal 'small' villages in the county Much Hadham is certainly the best looking, from an architectural point of view, of the larger villages or as Pevsner puts it: 'Of its own kind, Much Hadham is visually probably the most successful village in the county' and 'the main street is a delight from beginning to end.'

Above all it has an opulent look about it which no doubt stems from the fact that the Bishops of London had a Palace here from as early as the end of the 10th century, although the present building is basically a 17th century refacing of an earlier timber-framed 16th century building. The Palace stands at the north side of the churchyard and is now converted into flats, but the various Palaces over the centuries have seen much history. It is on record that Edmund Tudor was born here circa 1430, who in turn was the father of Henry VII, who became the first Tudor king after defeating Richard III at Bosworth Field in 1485.

There is so much to see here – mainly, of course, only from the outside – that a full village guidebook is necessary, but this is not the place for a house-to-house inventory. Although these are all private residences with all behind the facade hidden away, a walk up and down the main street, nearly a mile in length from one end to the other, is a very satisfying experience. At the north end there is The Lordship, a large mansion, complete with a fine stable block with its clock cupola, then a rich variety of 17th and 18th century cottages, with pargetting and half-timbering very much in evidence on some, but hidden on others until another mansion, Moor Place of circa 1775 is reached. On the way, one of the most interesting is the 7-bayed White House, all Gothicized now but, like so many in Much Hadham, a much older interior of circa 1600 is hidden behind the 19th century front. Nearby is the 16th century Morris Cottage with its exposed timbers.

And so to St. Andrew's where you are greeted by 'This is

the Gate to Heaven' over the door, and where there are two carved 'head stops' of a king and queen on the tower doorway by the late Henry Moore, the sculptor, who used to live in Much Hadham. Many centuries older, there are corbels with gargoyle-like faces and beasts, even Edward III holding a sceptre, helping to hold up the roof of the 15th century nave and north aisle.

There is much of the 15th century here including the font, the pulpit, the screen and some of the seating but the oldest treasures are some 13th century ironwork on the oak door leading into the vestry, and the remains of some wall-paintings of the same century on the blocked lancet window in the chancel.

Munden, Great & Little

Great Munden, and adjacent Nasty, hardly make up a village between them but the church has some interesting features whilst you can hardly overlook a place with a name like Nasty! There used to be a name-board but perhaps they became ashamed of it, although how could anyone be ashamed of this little hamlet of thatched cottages with names like The Swallows Nest? Actually Nasty, is a diminution over the years of 'at the east enclosure' according to *The Place-Names of Hertfordshire*.

The tower of the church is 15th century but there is the remains of the Norman chancel arch of circa 1120 and over the Jacobean pulpit one of the capitals has a face on it. In the south aisle two huge tomb recesses with ogee tops, and at the east end of the aisle an unusual stone reredos, also with ogee tops, dating from the early 15th century. In the Plough Inn there is an organ which was removed from the Gaumont Cinema, North Finchley: concert music has been recorded here for broadcasting on the Radio 2 *The Organist Entertains* programme.

Further south Little Munden is now bigger than Great Munden although the OS map does not even show the name

– but it does mark the position of the church of All Saints which dates back to 1100. Little Munden parish is made up of a number of hamlets of which Dane End has now become a popular village for commuters in this rather open stretch of country to the west of the A10 south of Buntingford. Note the two lodges just to the north of the northern Puckeridge roundabout on the A10, designed by Sir John Soane in 1783 for Hamels Park. Hamels Park mansion survives along with the 18th century stables, complete with clock turret, as the headquarters of a building concern with a new entrance, but the lodges now lead to what is the East Herts Golf Club and its modern clubhouse.

Newnham

➤ The Little Guide of 1903 is of the opinion that the interior of St. Vincent's church 'can show little of interest', but in 1963 a wall painting of St. Christopher fording a stream full of fishes was found on the north wall of the nave.

Newnham, watered by the unusually named Cat Ditch, is not much more than a hamlet consisting of a few cottages facing the church fashioned from the 17th century malting house of the old manor, a clutch of modern houses behind a green and Newnham Hall. Sad to say that there has not been a pub here since about 1900!

Reginald Hine, the Hitchin historian and author of a number of books about the Hitchin area and Charles Lamb, was born at the Hall and in the church there is a tapestry put up in his memory after his death in 1949, worked in the style of 1500.

Just about a mile to the north-west is the even smaller hamlet of Caldecote. Here is St. Mary Magdalene, the 14th century church of the original deserted village, now abandoned and derelict alongside barns which seem to be likewise.

In the porch however, is the finest holy water stoop in the county which is covered by a carved and crocketed canopy –

'an elaborate piece of work for a church in so remote a spot' (Tompkins in 1902). Unfortunately it may not now be possible to get at it to view it.

North Mymms or Mimms

◄━━ St Mary's church, North Mymms, celebrated its 750th anniversary in 1987 but you will look in vain on the OS map for a village marked 'North Mymms', despite the fact that it is there, as large as life, in Domesday Book as Mimmine. North Mymms, in fact, is a scattered rural parish comprising Welham Green, Bell Bar, Water End, Raestock and Little Heath with St. Mary's, physically separated from the community at large by the A1(M) actually in the grounds of North Mymms Park.

North Mymms House was built circa 1600, a few years before Hatfield House, but apparently designed by the same architect, Robert Lyminge, who went on to design Blickling Hall in Norfolk. But, as the *Shell Guide to Hertfordshire* says 'visitors are not encouraged', do not tarry at the octagonal lodge guarding the gates but hurry into the church, which is much older than the house.

The earliest remaining part is the chancel of the 13th century, whilst the nave and the aisles were all rebuilt as early as 1340 when a central tower was planned but never completed. Today's west tower, with new gargoyles of 1970 replacing 500 year old ones, is of the 15th century but has a 14th century doorway with carved flowers in the hollows, and a window over it which must have been moved from the old west wall.

There seems to be confusion as to the age of the pulpit. It is either very late Elizabethan or very early Jacobean, but otherwise the brasses and monuments are the interesting items here including a magnificent brass in the chancel, of a priest, Thomas de Horton, the vicar here in circa 1360.

The Mymmshall Brook, which flows alongside the main

road, disappears underground in what are called 'swallow holes' at Water End, and these are of great geological interest to the Thames Water Authority and the Nature Conservancy Council. Not a lot can be said otherwise about this area except for the extraordinary event of 15th September 1784! Welham Green's sole claim to fame is that balloonist Vincent Lunardi touched down here on that day on his historic flight, the earliest flight of any kind over British soil, on his way to Standon Green End (see High Cross). He dropped out of the sky over some astonished country folk and handed out his air-sick cat and rose again. At what is now called Balloon Corner at the junction of three roads, Dellsome Lane, Parsonage Lane and Huggins Lane, a commemorative stone was placed in 1960 – just 176 years after the event!

Northaw

➤ For the record Northaw WI is the oldest in Hertfordshire having been founded in 1917, although the area bounded by Northaw and Newgate Street is historic Enfield Chace, one of the hunting grounds of James I especially when he was staying at Theobalds (see Cheshunt).

Old cottages and some of the big houses which are not open to visitors remain because this is commuter territory now. However, Northaw Great Wood fashioned out of the remains of Enfield Chace is a Country Park owned and maintained by the County Council for the benefit of all.

Standing by the green with its old village pump is the church of St. Thomas the Martyr which has no history and is, as Pevsner writes, 'in its rock facing, its pinnacles on the west tower and its flowing tracery quite alien in the county'. It has no history because in 1881 it replaced another destroyed by fire which itself had only replaced an earlier one in 1809, but some plate including a Stuart chalice survived even though most of the old registers perished.

On the ground beside the tower with its four pinnacles is

another pinnacle on which is a plaque which reads 'This pinnacle belonged to the Second Church which stood on this site 1809–1881 when it was blown down'.

Northchurch

▬ Formerly called 'Berkhampstead St. Mary', and the original borough in Saxon times before a new community grew up around Berkhamsted castle and stole the name, Northchurch is, although virtually a continuation of its larger neighbour, still a village to many.

With new housing and shops gradually drifting along old Akeman Street, the church and its immediate vicinity is our concern here. There are several 15th and 16th century half timbered and brick cottages with the most important being the 16th century church almshouses by the church entrance. Inside the churchyard near the church porch is a gravestone

The Grave of Peter the Wild Boy at Northchurch

to 'Peter the Wild Boy 1785' and inside the church is a brass to his memory. He was found wandering wild without speech in a forest near Hanover in 1725, and after George I heard about it whilst on a visit, he took him back to England. Despite all efforts to teach him, he was placed in the care of farmers in Northchurch until he passed away in 1785.

The church itself has pre-conquest walls to the nave although the original Saxon tower has gone, now replaced by a central tower of the 15th century. There is an unremarkable 15th century font but a fine chest of circa 1500 with fine carvings, which is Flemish.

Nuthampstead

➤ A large scattered hamlet between Anstey and the Essex border which, formerly quietly remote, was rudely pitchforked into the 20th century when an American Bomber Base was laid across its fields in the Second World War (see Anstey). The old runway was broken up after it was rejected as the site for London's third airport, and thankfully the area has now reverted to its agricultural pursuits. No church here but outside the Woodman you will find a memorial to the 378th Heavy Bombardment Group USAF which was erected in 1983.

Offley

➤ Here is another village saved from constant traffic by the construction of a bypass linking Luton and Hitchin, so you can take breath more easily whilst looking at the village.

In the middle of the village Offley Place still stands as an Education Centre with one wing built circa 1600, but the rest was rebuilt in 1806 in a Gothic style. In the 18th century it was the home of Sir Thomas Salusbury, Judge of the High Court of the Admiralty who died in 1773. He was the uncle of Miss Hester Salusbury who spent a lot of her childhood here – she afterwards became Mrs. Thrale and a friend of Dr. Johnson. This same Sir Thomas was responsible for remodelling the chancel with a skylight and note that although it is apsed inside, it is square outside.

There are a number of fine monuments in the church including one huge one to Sir Thomas and his wife, but the real treasure is the 14th century font, which Arthur Mee calls 'one of the most beautiful in Hertfordshire'. There is a story about Sir Thomas and his wife, Sarah, retold by Branch Johnson which indicates a kindly and romantic nature. According to a family tradition, Sir Thomas' original engagement was broken but, some time later, the two of them, unbeknown to each other, took shelter from a storm under the same oak tree. Before the storm was over, they were once more engaged and the oak tree figures on their monument in the church.

There are a number of old cottages and inns on the west side of the bridge. Westbury Farm circa 1600 still contains a brick and timber dovecote of the 17th century.

Oxhey

'Oxhey is a hamlet on the Middlesex border' says my Little Guide of 1903, when Justice James Altham's chapel of 1612, built on the site of a much earlier house of prayer, was surrounded only by trees near to farm buildings. Nearby stood Oxhey Place, built on the site of Judge Altham's house which was demolished in 1688, from which came the oak used for the reredos in the chapel.

Since the Second World War, however, all changed when the old LCC built the huge housing estate in the grounds of Oxhey Place, albeit with a plan to preserve the mansion and other buildings for community use. Good intentions maybe, but Oxhey Place was burnt down in 1955 and all the other buildings disappeared soon after. All that is, except the chapel which now stands by the 1953 All Saints church which Pevsner rather unkindly calls a 'particularly ugly church'. It is to be hoped that Oxhey will do all in its power to preserve its one ancient monument, one which is very nearly the oldest building in the whole of the Watford area as well.

Out of the estate, and a short way along the A4125 to Rickmansworth, a farm can be seen down a track on the right hand side of the road. This is Oxhey Hall Farm which is, basically, a century older than the chapel and the OS map shows that there is a moat beside it. Very interesting but as it is a working farm and not in the public domain, it hardly qualifies for the accolade of Ancient Monument. I can verify that there is practically nothing to be seen of the moat now but it will always be on record.

Piccotts End

My 1903 Little Guide to the County has this entry – 'Piccotts End is passed when going from Hemel Hempstead to Great Gaddesden. It is on the river Gade at the NE extremity of Gadesbridge Park'.

Until 1953 no other guidebook would, probably, even have mentioned it and you would indeed have 'passed' through without a second thought. All this changed in 1953 when, in one of a row of 15th century cottages, a fine collection of medieval wall paintings depicting Christ and various saints were discovered in excellent preservation. The country's leading expert, Mr. Clive Rouse, dates them circa 1500, and it is suggested that the house was a pilgrims' hostel at one time.

At the time of writing, there was serious doubt as to their future due to the expense of upkeep but viewing may once again be possible at some future date.

Pirton

➤ First impressions in this ancient village, Peritone in Domesday Book, are probably correct: St. Mary's church is on the edge of what closer inspection will reveal as the remains of a motte and bailey castle known as Toot Hill. On the map it appears that the village is loosely scattered around an open space, and thus it has been since Norman Ralph de Limesie built his castle. Of course, no timber or masonry remains but approaching the church from the south, you must trace a path through the site.

Immediately by the north entrance of the church is a small half-timbered cottage, and this sets the tone for the village where a number of attractive farmhouses of 16th or 17th century remain, together with the village pond.

The nave of the church is of the 12th century, as well as the chancel, but the original tower of the same date collapsed in 1874. It was rebuilt in 1876 with a spike, using some of the original materials and there was a general restoration in 1883. The south doorway and south porch which is two storeyed, is circa 1360 – note that the porch is the only flint-built part of the church.

Inside there is a tablet with a curious inscription to Jane Docwra who died in 1645. She was the widow of Sir Thomas Docwra (see Lilley) who built High Down circa 1599 or a year or two later. High Down lies about a mile south of the church, between the Icknield Way and the village and, although not open or easily seen, is a fine example of a stone built late Elizabethan mansion.

Do not miss, however, the moated Pirton Grange of the same period complete with a timber-framed gatehouse over the moat. It is some two miles north-west of the village, right on the Bedfordshire boundary and apparently part of Shillington village, but it is much more viewable from the road.

Potten End

➤ There has been much speculation in local history circles over how this village came by its name, but whatever its origins, the name Potten End is here to stay! To many it may be just a more pleasant country link between Hemel Hempstead and Berkhamsted instead of the main road, but spare a moment to contemplate the traditional village scene with its pond on the green and pub, although most of the housing is modern plus a Victorian church in this now rather larger village. Grim's Ditch (see also Wigginton) starts more or less just to the west of the green whilst a mile or two due north, at Nettleden, a little hamlet between Great and Little Gaddesden, there is a 15th century tower on a church mainly of 1811.

Potters Bar

➤ Taken into the county in 1964 making, like the placing of Barnet in Greater London, the boundary line more sensible, Potters Bar has not much that is hidden. On the contrary the tall office blocks make it all rather conspicuous, especially from the M25! There are a few surprises, though, so let us begin with Wyllyotts Manor in Darkes Lane near the station.

There are council offices here leading off from the car park but the manor house of the 17th century with part of a much restored timber-framed barn of circa 1500 is now a bar and restaurant.

Darkes Lane itself was a country lane as recently as the early 1920s but the High Street was part of the old Great North Road so there you will find 17th century The Green Man and The Robin Hood of circa 1730.

Between Potters Bar and South Mimms, which used to be much larger than the original little hamlet of Potters Bar, there are several isolated farms of the 16th and 17th centuries but it is south down the A1000 (the old A1) that you should go to see the entrance to Wrotham Park. The house, which has featured in at least one TV thriller, may not be open to the public but two lodges and a gateway, which were neglected for many years, were restored and turned into dwellings in 1974–5. It will be noted that the lodges bear some resemblance to the Horse Guards sentry boxes in Whitehall. The sentry boxes in Whitehall were designed in 1742 by William Kent and the similarity can be explained by the fact that Isaac Ware, the architect of Wrotham Park was a great admirer of Kent's work.

Preston

➤ On the site of a Community house of the Knights Templars, and after 1312 of the Knights Hospitallers, the present Temple Dinsley dates from 1714 but was so much enlarged by Lutyens in 1908 that it all appears to be of that date. In 1935 it became a girls boarding school so, unless you have daughters and a yearning for private education, we cannot go in.

Concentrate instead on the pretty little village with its green, on which stands the old village well showing its iron mechanism under an octagonal roof, and a general clean and tidy aspect which has, on occasion, won it The Best Kept Smaller Village Trophy.

Inside the church is a 13th century coffin lid on which is a cross in relief. This was dug up at Temple Dinsley and no doubt covered one of the ancient Knights. St. Martin's church itself was only built in 1900 but a mile or so to the east on rising ground are the ruins of Minsden chapel, probably of the 14th century and derelict since the 17th century. To the north of the village is Wain Wood where in a hollow still called Bunyan's Dell, John Bunyan used to draw the crowds.

Puckeridge

➤ Before the bypass, Puckeridge lay on the route of Ermine Street, the old North Road, but now it is much quieter although some of the old inns which used to cater for the coaches in times past have remained. The Crown and Falcon is dated circa 1530 and it is possible that this was the inn at which Samuel Pepys stayed in 1662 on his way to Cambridge. It may well have been because of its age, and it is known that Pepys had a liking for Puckeridge, he visited the village on more than one occasion

Another old inn at the northern end of the village is The White Hart where the original road used to divide, Ermine Street continuing on to Royston whilst the road which Pepys would have taken to Cambridge via Barkway and Barley, forked off to the north east. The junction is still there but, because of the bypass, the link is a little more complicated now.

There is no establishment church here, the nearest one being at Standon, but a number of the houses in the village despite more modern additions, are as old as the inns and worthy of a closer inspection. At the southern end, in contrast to the remark above, there is a little 19th century Roman Catholic chapel with a Gothic look and further south off the main road, St. Edmund's College, a Roman Catholic public school which has been there since 1769. Pugin built them a chapel and some other buildings between 1845 and 1853 – Pugin was co-architect of the Houses of Parliament.

Puttenham

➤ Tempted to include Puttenham in with very near neighbour Long Marston, I decided that this tiny village, the most westerly in the county, deserved better, partly because of its age – entered in Domesday Book as Puteham with two mills – and partly because of the church of St. Mary.

First, with more and more churches being kept locked when no service or ceremony is being performed, it is a pleasure to congratulate the wardens here on putting up a rare sensible notice concerning the location of the keys! Inside it is a church full of surprises but the most unusual feature is a marble plaque on one wall which shows that Puttenham is a 'Thankful Village', the only one in the county and one of only 30 in the whole country. The plaque records that in the Great War of the years 1914–1918, this parish then numbering 71 souls sent forth and welcomed home all 15 men whose names are inscribed on the plaque. The inscription is rounded off:

'For their Gallant Service and their safe return
THANKS BE TO GOD'.

No need for a war memorial here and the community is so small that it would have been a problem to know where to put one except in the churchyard, and for the same reason it must be difficult for the churchgoers to maintain and look after their ancient 14th century building with a list of rectors going back to the 13th century. The tower has a stair turret higher than the parapet, the chancel is lower than the nave, the hexagonal 17th century pulpit has sea serpents or even Jonah's whale carved on it but the glory of the church is the almost flat 15th century roof of the nave. It has moulded beams enriched with bosses of flowers and shields. Angels are on the ends of the beams, and the roof rests on eight saints standing on the shoulders of quaint birds.

Radlett

In The Little Guide published in 1903 the author writes, that 'seen left from the train the neighbourhood is very pretty'. Although Radlett today is a very desirable residential area, I do not think that the author, could he return, would find the comment still to be very apposite.

The chief interest is the old Roman Watling Street passing through as the one main street, originally part of the A5 but now 'detrunked' as the A5183. This crosses the M25 near the disused Handley Page aerodrome buildings (now offices and warehouses) and one of Sir George Gilbert Scott's early church designs at Frogmore on its route to St. Albans.

The shops flanking both sides of the main road are unattractive and singularly out of keeping with the area, but there are still some flint and brick 'Gothick' cottages of 1852 by the station approach to remind us of the 'pretty' neighbourhood.

Radwell

➤ Radwell, tight up against the Bedfordshire border just like Holwell, is barely a hamlet and only approached by going under the A1(M) from the old Baldock Road but earns its place because of its wonderful 'lake', and unassuming but ancient All Saints church.

The river Ivel flows in from Bedfordshire and here at Radwell it suddenly becomes a lake in front of the now disused 19th century mill. It is a veritable bird-watcher's paradise with nothing to disturb the peace and quiet.

No tower or spike on the church, only a rather attractive little bell-cote over the west end of the nave, but the chief interest lies in the sculptures and brasses of three centuries. The most interesting of these is a nearly life-size alabaster monument to Mary Plomer, the first wife of William Plomer, who died aged 30 giving birth to her 11th child in 1605. Her baby lies in swaddling clothes beside her whilst at her feet kneel the other 10 children. Close by is William Plomer himself dressed in his armour along with his second wife. Someone had to look after the children!

Reed

➤ Three miles south of Royston and just off Ermine Street, the site of a Roman camp, Reed certainly was well established as Rete in Domesday Book. It has traces of six moats, some now little more than ponds, from the time when men sought security by surrounding their fortified houses with water. Even now, there is no village street as such, because the thatched and half-timbered buildings are scattered around three greens.

It is the antiquity of the church which earns it a place here. Standing somewhat isolated from the rest of the straggling village, the angles of the nave and the now blocked up north doorway are all of the early 11th century. The little church was restored in 1864 but the 15th century tower was left untouched.

Redbourn

➤ Redbourn finally got a bypass, after a long campaign, to take through traffic away from the High Street which is, in fact, part of Roman Watling Street. The bypass opened in 1984 and is much appreciated particularly when the M1 is blocked! Watling Street (the A5) was the busiest road in the whole country before the M1 was opened and, in the days of the stage coach, The Bull was an important staging post en route to the north-west. The three Georgian mansions of The Priory, The Red House and The Old Forge in the High Street are other reminders of coaching days but today the main centre of population lies to the west of Watling Street and the Common where there is now an ornamental village sign near the entrance to Church Street. The Common was once famous for its elm trees with Church End beyond being an interesting little entity almost on its own. In Church Street there is on the right The Hollybush Inn but on the left is the old workhouse with a dutch-gable roof and a contemporary plaque showing:

'This WorkHouse Rebuilt
Anno Domini 1790'

St. Mary's church is a real Norman antiquity with the massive square tower and the original nave dating back to circa 1170. Drawings still exist to show the old box pews and 3-decker pulpit but these were removed in 1850. The chief treasure now in a building which is not just an historic monument is the beautiful rood screen across the chancel arch of 1478, although the roodloft was destroyed in the Reformation.

The M1 thunders by just to the west of the church and immediately on the other side is the Aubreys Iron Age hillfort with the hotel, which takes its name from the site, built on part of it. It is not available for viewing so let us return to Watling Street and The Priory where there is a plaque on the wall which reads: 'Nearby this site stood Redbourn Priory dedicated to St. Amphibal in the 13th century. Several outbuildings to The Priory of a later date still survive in the vicinity'.

St. Amphibalus was the priest who was hidden by St. Alban, the act which ended in his martyrdom, who was himself reputedly put to death soon after on Redbourn Common. His reconstructed shrine is in the north chancel aisle of St. Albans Cathedral.

Rickmansworth

Rychemreworde in Domesday Book and in the charter granted by Henry VIII, Rykemeresworth meaning the 'rich land between the waters', Rickmansworth was well named because the rivers Colne, Gade and Chess unite here, with the Grand Union Canal threading its way through for good measure.

This ancient settlement, despite its proximity to Watford, the M25 and its housing estates, has several features of note but let us start with the church where there is not much of interest (I hasten to add 'architecturally') to keep us there. The tower of 1630 was retained when the whole building was rebuilt twice in the 19th century so it has the traditional battlements and spike, and there is a stone on the west face with the date on it. Brasses and monuments remain from the original building, the most important being the plain tomb chest containing both Robert Carey, the first Duke of Monmouth, and his son Henry. It was Robert Carey, the son of the earlier Henry who was a cousin of Queen Elizabeth I, who rode to Scotland after her death to tell James VI of Scotland that he was now King of England as well.

There are gargoyles on the tower but do not miss the stained glass east window with a Crucifixion by Burne-Jones, put in in 1896.

There are several houses around the church including the early 17th century Bury which is now used as offices, and the Priory, but just north of the church is perhaps the most historically interesting house in the town. This is Basing House, now used as Council offices and standing between the Library of 1968 and the Watersmeet Community Hall of 1975. Not open, of course, to the public except on business, it is the site of the house that the former Quaker statesman and founder of Pennsylvania, William Penn and his wife, lived in for five years after their marriage in 1672. The present house was built in 1740, and there are public gardens and a bowling green at the rear of the house. It may be of interest to recall that William Penn is buried in the little churchyard at Jordan's Meeting House in Buckinghamshire.

In the other direction, south of the church, is Batchworth Lock on the Grand Union Canal which, in the summer, attracts many onlookers and nearby is the aquadrome and water-skiing etc.

Finally, only about a mile away from the town is Moor Park, 'the grandest 18th century mansion in Herts' (Pevsner), which is now the prestigious clubhouse for a golf-club but open for viewing at certain times. The south entrance facing Batchworth Heath is still dominated by lodges and a central Roman Doric archway, the scene of one of the incidents in the famous film *Genevieve*.

Ridge

◤ A tiny hamlet, part, apparently, of a parish which stretches all the way from Colney Heath to Bignells Corner with the M25 tearing through the middle of it. The building of the motorway obliterated The Waggon and Horses on Ridge Hill, at one time a haunt of highwaymen but in more recent times the very first hostelry in the now considerable Trust House Forte empire.

The sleepy hamlet which appears to have been overlooked by the developers (so near the M25 can it only be a matter of time?) is notable for just two particulars, one being very unexpected. Opposite the church is Orchard Mead. Converted into a house in 1950, it was originally a block of five almshouses designed by Sir George Gilbert Scott in circa 1850.

St. Margaret's church, rebuilt of flint in the 15th century although there is evidence of an earlier building on the site, has a low embattled tower with a large defaced 15th century St. Christopher wall painting on the north wall of the nave. The surprise is outside.

One of the greatest of the Second World War commanders, although an Irishman, chose to be buried in an area where he had property. Field Marshal the Earl Alexander of Tunis, along with his wife, lies buried under the trees in the quiet churchyard.

Royston

➤ The Little Guide asserts that 'Royston is a somewhat quaint town, with some narrow byways and odd-looking houses', but nothing is so odd as the cave which lies virtually beneath what used to be the main crossroads in the town where the Icknield Way crossed Ermine Street.

Accidentally rediscovered in 1742 by workmen who were digging a hole in what was then the Butter Market, the bottle-shaped cave which has no equal, certainly not in this country, was found to be full of rudely carved reliefs of the Crucifixion, St. Christopher, kings, queens etc. of all sizes and ages. Controversy has raged ever since as to the purpose, the age and who dug it, but no matter. Open Saturday and Sunday between Easter and September, so go and enjoy a unique experience.

On the crossing itself is a two-ton boulder called the 'Royse Stone' which was the base for a cross now long gone, placed there, it is said, by a Lady Roysia and which gave the place its first name. Although you cannot cross here now because of the blocked off High Street, this stone serves as a constant reminder of the centuries-old importance of this ancient junction.

A few hundred yards north along what is Kneesworth Street is what is known as The Palace, in reality all that remains of King James I's hunting lodge. You cannot miss it on account of the huge chimneys down to street level with an attractive shell-hooded door between them. It appears that the King took a fancy to Royston after spending three days with the lord of the manor in 1603 when he was travelling to London from Scotland to claim his throne after the death of Queen Elizabeth.

He had the Palace built and often came to hunt and shoot on Royston Common, although his visits were not at all popular with the townsfolk – it became very expensive for them! It was while he was in residence at Royston that he signed the death warrant of Sir Walter Raleigh – it is said just to please the Spanish Ambassador!

The King's Palace at Royston

In the other direction, south of the blocked-off road, are a number of houses of several centuries but note particularly the 1849 courthouse with its coat of arms – now a travel agency!

The church of St. John the Baptist is, in fact, a survival of part of the large church of a monastery of Augustinian Canons founded near the crossroads in 1162 and developed as the parish church after the Reformation. During restoration in 1872 fragments of a former screen were made into a pulpit and reading desk. The church is of great interest because of its history and the excellence of the earlier details, especially the lancet windows of circa 1250 in the nave, which were only discovered during the 1872 restoration. Also noticeable is the alabaster effigy of a knight circa 1415 with two angels at his head. Of the same period are the 15th century alabaster images of the Virgin and a bishop – both headless.

Rushden

➤ The Moon and the Stars may tempt you to stop after returning from Wallington but, after noting the pargetting on the nearby cottage, resist the temptation until you have had a look at the 'pretty' village of Rushden which lies just off this minor road.

The road actually leads nowhere but, as Pevsner says, there are 'many very neatly kept cottages in the scattered village' and some of these are half-timbered and thatched.

St Mary's church has a 19th century chancel and south porch but essentially it belongs to the 15th century. However, although the south porch was built circa 1849, the south doorway itself is of the 14th century. There is a 15th century font here and several memorials to members of the Meetkirke family, including one to Sir Adolphus Meetkirke who lived at Julians (mainly 20th century now but originally of the 16th century) and was sometime the Ambassador from Flanders to the Court of Queen Elizabeth I.

Sacombe

➤ Although sandwiched between the Watton-at-Stone to Ware road and the A10, Sacombe today appears as remote as anywhere in the county even though it appears in Domesday Book as Seuechampe. It is, however, worth a small diversion for several reasons.

The little church of St. Catherine, partly hidden by trees, lies between Sacombe and Sacombe Green, which are connected by what the OS map marks as a Roman road. The church was rebuilt in 1865 and much of the restoration was done with materials brought from the demolished church at Thundridge, and is now architecturally of little interest apart from its tower with a low stair turret. Inside are two good monuments by two of the foremost sculptors of their period, one by Rysbrack in 1758 and the other by Flaxman in 1815.

At Sacombe Green there is what Pevsner calls 'an exceptionally picturesque timber-framed 15th–17th century house, carefully restored in the 20th century': it is well worth making the effort.

St. Albans

➤ H. M. Alderman in his book *A Pilgrimage in Hertfordshire*, published in 1931, wrote: 'Is there a more historically interesting place in England than the City of St. Albans? Probably not'. Many other historic towns and cities would, no doubt, dispute this but there can be no argument about St. Albans being the most important historic centre in the county. At the same time there can be no doubt that there are more books, pamphlets and brochures about Verulamium, the city and the cathedral than about any other locality in the county so there is no need to repeat what is so readily available.

Bear with me should I tell you about some feature which may be fully written up in your other guidebooks but let us look at a few oddities and antiquities which are, to all intents and purposes, 'hidden' or which are, at least not in the spotlight.

The medieval Clock Tower, which was built between 1403 and 1412 and is unique except for one other in Morpeth, Northumberland, dominates the Market Place but take a look back along the wall above the shop names towards the Laura Ashley shop and there is a stone urn in a niche nearly opposite the 17th century Boot Inn. This appears to be the site of a long-lost market pub – the urn is the traditional emblem of the New Inn. Further along, the Laura Ashley shop is a good timber house of the early 17th century and note the date '1637' embossed on one of the upper gables which is repeated on the more modern rain-water head.

Opposite note the stone tablet recording the building of the Corn Exchange in 1857 but what you are looking at is the top of the actual Corn Exchange itself. The Corn Exchange was built in 1857 but when it became redundant, the whole of the west side was cut away below the cornice in the mid 1920's and shops were built as seen today.

Above the entrance to Christopher Place is a rather splendid clock but instead of entering the shopping precinct, look down French Row. Forget the shops and you still have the real look of the Middle Ages complete with overhangs etc. At the lower end, between the Fleur de Lys and what was the Christopher Inn (which gave the name to the new precinct) there is an archway which leads to the rear of Christopher Place. At the other side, on one of the posts supporting the overhanging upper storey, and acting like a corbel, is a wooden female form with a somewhat generous figure.

The Victoria History of Hertfordshire states that there are similar figures in the Waxhouse Gate Alley but that was in 1908, there is nothing to be seen now. The Waxhouse Gate itself, supposedly built by Sir Christopher Wren's master mason, remains as a metaphorical link between city and cathedral.

A few feet after turning left at the bottom of George Street there is a raised path leading to the cathedral slightly above the road to the Gatehouse of circa 1360, and you will at once see three and a half worn steps which lead to nothing but a brick wall. Above is a plaque which reads 'Original Entrance to Upcot House anno 1761'. Apparently there was a Methodist Meeting House at one time but it is unknown when it was no longer used for that purpose and enquiries have elicited stories of a storehouse and a carpenter's shop during the present century. Whatever may have been there, there is nothing to see now except steps that lead nowhere!

There is one antiquity in St. Albans which, although mentioned in the guidebooks but not in detail, surely deserves a place here and that is Ye Olde Fighting Cocks Inn which stands by the lake in Verulamium Park. At one time it was claimed that the Fighting Cocks in Abbey Mill Lane was 'the oldest inhabited house in England' but, as the author of *Picturesque Hertfordshire* wrote 85 years ago, 'this must be regarded with suspicion!'.

This claim has, of course, long been dropped and although there is no disputing the antiquity of this attractive building, a sign on the wall proclaims:

'The Old Round House Rebuilt after the Flood of 1599. This famous Octagon was originally a medieval pigeon house c. 1400 re-erected here as a House in 1600 on the site of St. Germains Gate. Part of the Monastery founded by King Offa of Mercia c. 798 it became the local centre for Cockfighting in the 17th and 18th centuries but was re-named The Fisherman when this sport became illegal in 1849'

Leaving the cathedral and the massive Gatehouse to the guidebooks, you must see the outside of No 13 Fishpool Street with its remains of what was once much more elaborate pargetting, before taking a look at the variety of old houses and cottages all the way down this, the most attractive street in the city – unfortunately ruined by the ubiquitous motor car. Past the Kingsbury Mill, now a museum, up St. Michael's Street and at the top is the church of St.

Michael. Here in the chancel is the famous life size statue of Sir Francis Bacon, apparently comfortably asleep, and there is a fine carved Jacobean pulpit with a rare hour glass and still with its tester. Note also the 15th century 'Doom' of wood now preserved on the south wall of the nave. It is but a remnant but the only one in the county.

Away from St. Michael's, past the Roman Theatre, along the drive to and past Gorhambury House and you come to Old Gorhambury House, the surviving remains of a mansion built by Sir Nicholas Bacon, the father of Sir Francis, in 1563–1568. This building was much favoured by Queen Elizabeth I and it is on record that she once said to Sir Nicholas, 'My Lord, your house is too little for you'. His happy reply to this was as follows: 'No, Madam, but 'tis your Highness has made me too great for my house!'. It is now under the control of English Heritage and open at any reasonable time.

Finally, back south-east over the city to what is known as Cottonmill Lane, a long road linking two parts of London Road with a big sweep across the Verulam golfcourse, past the 18th century Sopwell House (now a hotel), Cottonmill itself and then, in an open space opposite the end of Prospect Road, the most unsung ruins in the city!

In 1140 Sopwell Nunnery was founded for nuns previously attached to the Abbey, but it was destroyed after the Dissolution. Sir Richard Lee, who was a royal engineer and surveyor, built a mansion on the site retaining the monastic ground plan and using the old materials. Over the centuries, guides have often referred to the ruins mistakenly as being of the actual nunnery and today they stand neglected, surprisingly without graffiti but without a signboard or noticeboard to their name!

St. Ippollitts

➤ A humorous poem by Lorin Knight, printed in the County magazine in 1976 goes like this:

'Who is the quaintly christened Saint
Who must take all the blame
For giving so pretty a village
So preposterous a name?
No doubt he chuckles loud and long
No doubt he is in fytts
At fools like me who struggle so
To spell St. Ippolytts

Even back in history
They seem to have had fights
Over whether it was Hippolitts,
Pollets or Epolites.
Oh, please, can someone help before
I bight my pen to bbyts;
Oh, please, can someone tell me how
to spell St. Ippollytes?'

It had to be printed complete so that the full flavour could be enjoyed, but I have settled here for the OS version. Whatever the spelling, the church is one of only two in England dedicated to St. Hippolytus, an eminent bishop and theologian who lived in the 3rd century and it was founded in 1087 by Judith, the niece of the Conqueror, who went on to become the prioress of the Benedictine priory at Elstow in Bedfordshire.

The church is situated on top of a hill so it can be seen from quite a distance, particularly the embattled tower complete with spike. It was almost entirely rebuilt between 1877 and 1878 from the foundations, but much use was made of old materials and an original Norman window of the 11th century can be found on the south wall. There is, however, no shrine to the worthy St. Hippolytus, the patron saint of horses and a great deal of doubt exists as to his real identity. The village took its name from the saint, nevertheless, and you will notice that the signwriters or their masters have conflicting views on that spelling!

Near the church is a 17th century half-timbered private house with an overhang which was formerly the Olive Branch Inn, and on the B656 at the bottom of the hill is a 'gothick' thatched cottage called The Lodge.

A little to the west lies the hamlet of Gosmore and my Little Guide says simply, 'Gosmore is a small village. The nearest church is at Ippollitts'. Very true still to this day but note some interesting 17th and 18th century houses including Maydencroft Manor (shown on OS map) and The Bull, also of the 17th century.

St. Paul's Walden

◄━━ A plaque on the north wall of All Saints church reads as follows:

'The organ and this tablet were placed
in the church by a parishioner to the Glory of
God and in memory of the Coronation of Their
Majesties King George VI and Queen Elizabeth
May 12th 1937
Her Majesty Queen Elizabeth was born in this
Parish Aug 4 1900. Baptized in this Church
Sept 23 1900 and here worshipped'

Queen Elizabeth The Queen Mother did, indeed, spend much of her childhood at St. Paul's Waldenbury and certainly was baptized in the church. She was born, however, in London but the actual location remains a mystery.

The Bury is not open to the public but the wonderful gardens, one of the few formal gardens remaining in the county, are open on certain Sundays in the summer. The layout was begun in 1720 by Edward Gilbert, an ancestor of the Queen Mother, and he also designed the ornate screen in the church. He obtained sculptures and other 'garden furniture' from various sources, including the Lake Temple designed by Sir William Chambers.

North of the Bury, Sir Arthur Sullivan's one-time home, Stagenhoe (at one time a preparatory school) is now one of the Sue Ryder Homes with the main gates on the B651, but another narrow road leads back to the tiny village past the church. Gilbert's screen with its elaborate patterns leads into the chancel, and this is matched by the Lady Chapel on the south side which is about 200 years earlier. Obvious in the church are several memorials to the Bowes Lyon family, perhaps less so is the early 14th century Virgin and Child in the only medieval glass in the west tower window, hidden somewhat behind the organ.

Sandon

➤ The manor of Sandone was owned by Saxon kings and in Domesday Book was still shown as Sandone. This little village has not only a long history but the foundations of England's oldest known windmill, 14th century or early 15th century, were found on what is known as the Mount east of the church, although there is nothing to be seen above ground.

All Saints' church with its west tower propped up by huge ugly 17th century buttresses, a 16th century house with an overhang and the Six Bells make an attractive triangle atop one of the few hills in the county which overlooks most of the parish.

Old barns and a dovecote survive at Sandonbury just to the south of All Saints and the church holds other treasures – 15th century benches as well as a contemporary screen, Jacobean pulpit and a tiny Easter Sepulchre of an even earlier date.

Sandridge

➤ Each volume of the original *King's England* series of books by Arthur Mee covering the counties of England had this proud boast on the dust jacket: 'There have been many books on (whichever county it was) but never one like this'. If you know Arthur Mee's *Hertfordshire* of 1939, then you know the photograph of a little girl in a gymslip pumping water into a bucket from the village pump outside The Queen's Head with St. Leonard's church in the background in the unspoilt village of Sandridge.

The pump is long gone. Sandridge, well established even at the time of Domesday Book, now seems to be just an extension of St. Albans but, despite that and the huge estate of Jersey Farm, the place strives to maintain a village status.

Forget the Home Office's Research Station on Woodcock Hill off the road to Hatfield, just concentrate on the little triangle of the church, the Queen's Head and the one-time vicarage at 'Lyndon', now a Salvation Army Retirement Home.

St. Leonard's looks ordinary enough from outside but a surprise awaits you inside as well as a 12th century font and a stone pulpit. Although much restored in 1887, St. Leonard's has long passed its 850th anniversary. In the late 14th century a virtually unique stone screen was built incorporating the 12th century chancel arch of Roman bricks already there. The presence of these Roman bricks, not only in the screen arch but also in the walls of the church itself suggests a pre-Conquest date which is certainly not out of the question.

It is worthy of mention that the Duke of Marlborough's first title, on elevation to the peerage, was Baron Sandridge – and further, it is important to remember that the name is pronounced 'Sarndridge' by the locals!

Sarratt

➤ Complete with a strangely shaped pump which has not been in use since the early 1920s, the long and wide village green is the most prominent feature of a place which, despite its attractiveness in 'Metroland', has kept a village look. Houses and cottages grouped around the green with duck pond and the old 17th century Boot Inn make up an unspoilt traditional picture but this is, in truth, Sarratt Green.

The real Sarratt, now called Church End, is no doubt the original site and where stands the most untypically Hertfordshire church of the Holy Cross. Basically a flint Norman church of cruciform design, the tower has the only saddleback roof in the county, rebuilt, with Roman bricks incorporated, in the 15th century. Restored in 1866 by Sir George Gilbert Scott, a great deal was done without spoiling the antiquity of the church although he did replace the old box pews. The tower is untouched and puddingstone, built into its base and embedded here and there in the walls, helps to give a prehistoric origin to the site. Look for remains of wall paintings, and the 17th century pulpit with its tester or sounding board.

Opposite the church are The Baldwin Almshouses. These are dated 1821 by Pevsner but this was the date when they were rebuilt by Ralph Day, the original date is 1550 which makes them the earliest purpose-built almshouses in the county.

Sawbridgeworth

➤ Sabrixteworde in Domesday Book is recorded as having at least one mill, and the town prospered over the centuries from milling and malting. The weatherboarded mill buildings, including Burton's Mill, stand by the river

Stort although many are put to new uses: still a picturesque sight.

Unlike many large villages or small towns which have grown by expanding along a main road, Sawbridgeworth is basically a compact little place with a wealth of interesting 16th, 17th and 18th century buildings concentrated in Bell Street, Knight Street and Fair Green. A most comprehensive pamphlet is published with full details by the Bishops Stortford and District Local History Society but note particularly the Georgian 'Red House' in Bell Street and the 16th century Market House with its overhang in Knight Street.

Fair Green, with an air of elegant past, leads to several points of interest including Corner House with a 'Firemark' over the doorway and on the garden wall a plaque put up on 22nd August 1951 which reads 'This plaque was erected by the Sawbridgeworth Urban District Council to commemorate the transfer to the Council of the Manorial rights in the Fair Green which rights are the subject of a Charter granted by King Henry VI on the 13th February 1448'.

St. Mary's church is a large church and, unlike so many in the county, it is not embattled except for the west tower to which a low stair turret was added in the 16th century. An arch from the chancel to the south chapel gives a clue to its age, apparently of circa 1300, but there was extensive 19th century restoration with Sir George Gilbert Scott dealing with the chancel. However, there is still a font of 1400, a pulpit of 1632 and, in Pevsner's words, 'a veritable storehouse of monuments'.

Shenley

➤ The hospital occupies a commanding position here but it does not affect nor spoil the rural look of the village which, despite some modern blocks of flats (one called 'Forge Court' because it stands on the site of a blacksmith's forge which was still active in 1955 when I first knew Shenley) still has its pond, some thatched cottages and, above all, its cage or lock-up. Note the wording under the two little windows: 'Do Well and Fear Nought' and 'Be Sober, Be Vigilant'.

The core or main building of the hospital is the house built by Nicholas Hawksmoor, the famous architect who worked with Wren on St. Paul's Cathedral and with Vanbrugh at Castle Howard and Blenheim. This is Porter's Park – not, of course, open to the public – but Hawksmoor's modest tomb can be seen in the churchyard of what was St. Botolph's church, now converted to a private house.

Whilst on the search for Hawksmoor's tomb, note a most unusual headstone in the shape of Air Force wings on the grave of Captain Ronald Arbuthnot. He survived the duration of the First World War, first in the Army and then in the Royal Flying Corps, but, on a last flight out of the old London Colney airfield (between London Colney and Shenley) he crashed the plane and was killed on 3rd December 1918, just three weeks after the signing of the Armistice on 11th November 1918.

South Mimms

➤ My little 1903 guidebook states that South Mimms 'is prettily situated on rising ground' which sounds a little bizarre today when the M25 motorway is the dominant feature of this area. But all is not lost, and the district of South Mimms or Mymms (take your pick) has several things to offer the diligent searcher.

North of the village, up a minor road off Telford's original road (now A111) and amid the trees of Mymmshall Wood, are the remains of a motte and bailey castle of circa 1142, which was excavated between 1960 and 1967.

Back south and after careful negotiation of the complicated M25/A1 junction, you may ultimately find yourself on the A1081, the road to Barnet. Halfway along is a road known as Trotters Bottom, and immediately after turning into it the beautifully restored (in 1987) monumental gateway of Dyrham Park, complete with Tuscan Column and a low urn on top, comes into view. The estate is now a golf course but this restoration, after many years of neglect, must have given heart to all who strive to save our heritage from destruction.

Back in the village where you can escape from the traffic, the almshouses of 1856, maintained by an even older Charity, stand right next to St. Giles' church where there is much of interest. Originally a Middlesex church, there is no spike on the 14th century tower but there is a stair turret, and there is a staircase to the former rood loft preserved inside. By the 13th century font is a chest of the same period which Pevsner suggests is one of the oldest pieces of furniture in the county.

The most important name here is Frowyk. There are brasses and tombs of various members of the family but it was Henry Frowyk, a successful merchant, who paid for the north aisle and north chapel which were added in 1526. He lies in a grand canopied altar tomb of 1535.

Standon

➤ The detached church tower, unique in the county, and the large puddingstone lump opposite the former brick and timber school of the 16th century ensure that this village is not forgotten, but why such a wide street? Apparently it is a relic of the fact that it was granted a market charter as early as the 13th century, and was a market town to rival Ware. The Star and many of the houses in the street are of the 17th and 18th century, and collectively look most attractive.

South of the village proper and over a little ford is what is left of The Lordship, built in 1546 by the river Rib by Sir Ralph Sadleir who, in his old age, was appointed, albeit very reluctantly, as a custodian of Mary Queen of Scots by Queen Elizabeth. He died seven weeks after she was beheaded in 1587 and he is remembered, with his son Sir Thomas, by standing effigies in St. Mary's church. By the side of Sir

Ralph's effigy, which is in armour, are his helmets, a 14th century sword, spurs and a standard pole, said to have been captured from the King of Scotland at Musselburgh.

The last male Sadleir died in 1660, the year of the Restoration of the Monarchy, and he left the Lordship estate to his nephew, Lord Aston of Tixall which is in Staffordshire. He came to live at The Lordship and, although he was a most eccentric, not to mention greedy and gluttonous person, his house competed for some years with Hatfield House as the social centre of the county. Nearly two centuries later the house was bought by the Duke of Wellington, although he never appears to have lived in it, and in 1927 it was partly destroyed by fire.

Stanstead Abbots

St. Andrew's church on the Ware road, built within the present village only in 1880, is not the gem to look for here. Although it is the parish church now, it is the rarely used old church of St. James, now cut off from the village even more than before by the long-awaited bypass, that demands attention, but you may have to search for someone who holds the key.

It is a nearly perfect example of an ancient church still fitted with 18th century high box pews and a three-decker pulpit, unfortunately lacking its tester or sounding board. The north chapel was added by Sir Edward Baeshe in 1577 and there is a fine memorial on the chapel wall to him, his wife, a daughter of Sir Ralph Sadleir (see Standon), and his children. He died in 1587 and so he did not see the rout of the Spanish Armada in the following year. He would have been proud as he was not only lord of the manor at Stanstead but also 'General Surveyor of the Victuals for the Navy Royal and Marine affairs within the Realm of England and Ireland'.

A knight dressed in armour of the previous century, the century when the wooden south porch was erected, is

The Old Clock School at Stanstead Abbots

remembered in brass on a huge block of stone, but his name is not known.

Back in the village, at the foot of the hill stand the Baeshe Almshouses which were put up in the early 17th century by Sir Edward's son, another Sir Edward, who followed in his father's footsteps as lord of the manor at Stanstead Bury.

There are several large houses in the area but now most are converted to multifarious uses. Briggens is a country hotel, Netherfield House is a Salvation Army Home for retired gentlemen and Easneye is occupied by the All Nations College for Missionary students.

In the main street note Stanstead Hall, dated 1752 and a most unusual circular stair turret with an embattled top. Immediately to its right on the awkward right hand bend is the 17th century Red Lion, still looking much as it did in coaching days and opposite the final treasure of Stanstead Abbots – the Old Clock School built by Sir Edward Baeshe, the younger, circa 1636.

141

Stanstead St. Margaret

◣ The notorious level-crossing which foɪ decades caused traffic congestion at Stanstead Abbots strictly belongs to Stanstead St. Margaret, but now the bypass has changed all that and, if you dare stop on the busy road, the whole of this tiny neighbour of the larger village can be viewed from an elevated viewpoint.

The little flint church from which the village takes its name is very old with a nave of early 12th century, probably formed from one aisle of an even older edifice. Over the west end of the nave is a small bell turret and there are low box pews inside. There is a floor slab before the altar over the body of Henry Lawrence, a kinsman of Cromwell and a friend of Milton. After the Restoration he was permitted to live in the manor house, still with 18th century gates with heraldic crest, hard by the church, where he died in 1664. A very recent addition to this church, which is in the smallest parish in the county – in fact, a parish within the larger parish of Great Amwell – is a set of ten engraved glass panels depicting local scenes on a wooden memorial screen. The screen was dedicated by the Bishop of St. Albans in October 1987.

Just below the elevated bypass is The Clock House which was reconstructed from an 18th century stable gatehouse and is, as Pevsner says 'a pretty composition'. Nearby is an octagonal dovecote but on the Hoddesdon side of the bypass is a building which has a very mixed roofscape crowned by a tall clock turret with a spire, which has earned it the soubriquet as the oddest looking maltings in the county.

Stapleford

◣ This little hamlet which is barely noticed when driving along the A602 between Hertford and Stevenage deserves more because of its church. Pause awhile, cross the river Beane and St. Mary's church, seemingly mid-Victorian, turns out to have a nave of circa 1150 and even the chancel may be of the same date. There were all sorts of additions in 1874, including an unusual tower with a weather-boarded upper stage, but there is still a Norman doorway (blocked up) in the north wall with all the original characteristics of 1150.

Stevenage

◆━ Following the New Towns Act after the Second World War, Stevenage was the first New Town to be designated in November 1946 and guide books and brochures are available with the full story. It should not be overlooked, however that the town centre was one of the first traffic-free precincts to be built in Europe, and is embellished by a clock tower, fountain and the 'Joyride' sculpture by F. Belsky.

Historically speaking, the present Old Town was itself new when it moved away from the church in the 13th century to group itself round the Great North Road – the earliest settlement was around St. Nicholas'. Much of hidden Stevenage is in the Old Town, which in the 18th and 19th centuries was an important coaching stop. Many of the old buildings behind their present facades hide the remains of their former occupation of inns. No 5 High Street, 'The Grange', now the Education Offices and Registry Office, was one of these, formerly The Swan where Pepys once stayed. Very near is the original one room schoolroom of 1561, now the Headmaster's office, which developed into Alleynes School.

Stevenage Moat House, the uninspiring name given to what was the Cromwell Hotel, was once Home Farm which belonged to John Thurloe who was Cromwell's Secretary of State and Master Spy! The old farmhouse has been incorporated into the hotel and can still be clearly defined.

At the southern end of the High Street is the 1851 Holy Trinity church, by another old coaching inn, The Coach and Horses. Behind is the best timber-framed building in the

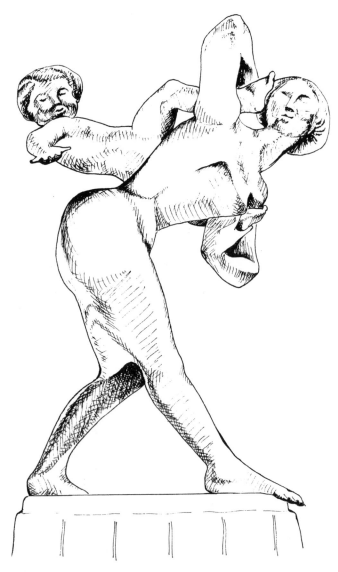

'Joyride' by Franta Belsky in Stevenage town centre

144

whole area at the beginning of Letchmore Road, 16th century and between 1773 and 1835 it was the workhouse.

And so to St. Nicholas' church, which dates mainly from 1150 although much altered circa 1350, leaving the tower as the oldest part of the building, with a spire added in the 15th century. There is an early 13th century square shaped font, and an effigy of a lady with hands raised in prayer in the north aisle but here, as at Anstey and Bishops Stortford, there is the rare treasure of six misericords in the chancel.

South of the town centre on what was the Old Great North Road is Stevenage's one true antiquity – the Six Hills, which are Romano-British barrows, but do not leave without looking for Shephall which certainly qualifies for being included in 'hidden Hertfordshire'. Completely encompassed by the New Town, Shephall is now the only 'neighbourhood' apart from the Old Town which incorporates an older settlement. The village green is carefully preserved and the little church of St. Mary, although much restored and rebuilt in 1956, has remains of the 14th century and a 15th century screen.

Stocking Pelham

➤ The route through Stocking Pelham provides the best link between the other two Pelhams, and although there is not a lot to see when driving through the sparsely populated countryside, Stocking Pelham – a name probably derived from 'a land covered by tree stumps' – right on the Essex border, is not without interest.

The unassuming little church lacks a tower and has a Victorian look about it as you approach but, in fact, it dates from the early 14th century with a list of rectors which goes back to 1333.

The Royal Commission tells us that there are 141 homestead moats in the county 'mostly on the eastern side'. The Rectory here, standing just to the east of the church, can still boast remains of its stirrup-shaped moat.

Tewin

➤ Tewin is one of a clutch of villages, like Datchworth, Bramfield and Digswell, which lies between the Hertford–Stevenage road and the Welwyn Garden City–Stevenage road, and is now very much a dormitory area. The village is divided into the Upper and Lower Green, with Lower Green being a good example of how modern commuter housing has been fused in with the existing cottages.

The Green was reconstructed to coincide with the celebrations planned for the Queen's Coronation in 1953, and the bus shelter there was formed out of an old well. The Rose and Crown is of the mid 18th century whilst The Plume of Feathers on the Upper Green is older, of late 16th or early 17th century vintage.

Tewin is notable for a number of large houses including the 1560 Queen Hoo, almost unaltered since built, and Tewin Water which is now a school for deaf children. Neither, of course, is open to the public so with a passing mention of Tewin House which was pulled down in 1807 it is the church of St. Peter, which remains rather isolated in what formerly was parkland around Tewin House, which is the focus of interest here.

The church has parts dating right back to the 11th century but the chancel is of the 13th century and the tower 15th. The south porch entrance is partly blocked by the monument to General Joseph Sabine, one time resident at Queen Hoo who died in 1739 after being Governor of Gilbraltar. In the churchyard is the altar tomb of Lady Anne Grimston who died in 1710. The tomb is split open by ash and sycamore trees growing together, a circumstance popularly attributed to her sceptical opinions. She is said to have denied the doctrine of immortality, and to have expressed the wish that such a phenomenon should happen if the doctrine were indeed true!

Inside the church is a memorial tablet to Lady Cathcart, who outlived four husbands and finally died 'in the 98th year of her age' at a previous house on the site where the present school for the deaf stands. The present Tewin Water, built in 1819, was acquired by the Beit brothers, who had been friends and financial collaborators with Cecil Rhodes in South Africa. They were originally Germans, born in Hamburg and after making their fortunes in Africa, settled in England after developing a great love for this country, and now lie peacefully side by side in St. Peter's churchyard.

Just to the east of Tewin Water is Tewin Bury Farm with its old barn, where accommodation is available – all part of the Hertfordshire Farm and Countryside Tourist Group which contains a dozen very different farms spread throughout the county.

Therfield

➤ Although the church looks like many an 'old' one, it was virtually a new one of 1875, incorporating some fragments and fillings of the old church dating from the 13th century, built on the original site. The tower was only added in 1911 but it has its spike like many much older churches.

Kept in the vestry or elsewhere, relics from the old church include: a slab with an incised cross, a 14th century stone on which the tiny figure of a recumbent man only about 10 inches high lies most uncomfortably between two even smaller female figures, and a large carved mural monument of cedarwood with carved figures of Death and Father Time with his hour glass and scythe.

There are a number of interesting houses, both brick and half-timbered, in the village, 'Old Forge' with its half-timbering and partly thatched roof being particularly attractive, but these, of course, are all private property. In passing, note that what was previously the rectory is partly 15th century, quite a rarity in the county for a secular building. On the other hand, do not leave Therfield without a sight of Tuthill Manor, a former nearly derelict barn with a date

147

traced back to 1480 and now converted to a luxury home which has been granted a listed building licence.

On nearby Therfield Heath are five burial mounds including the only long barrow in the county.

Thorley

➤ Until the 1970s, Thorley was mainly scattered along the A11 south of Bishops Stortford under the name of Thorley Street, whilst the church of St. James retained its rural charm alongside the 14th century Thorley Hall a mile or so to the west. Now a large housing development has changed all that although the church is still isolated as before at the end of a lane which ends by a village pond.

History has been remembered however, in some of the road names, in particular Whittington Way to remind us of Sir Richard Whittington (the famous 'Dick') who was lord of the manor from 1399 to 1413.

Thorley was one of the few places still to have its old stocks which were in the churchyard, but they are now in the museum at Bishops Stortford. Although St. James' was restored in 1854 and acquired a pulpit and communion rails by Sir George Gilbert Scott, it has a 12th century font and a marvellous example of Norman zigzag in the 12th century south porch.

Throcking

➤ The scattered hamlet of Throcking, down a turning opposite Buttermilk Farm a mile or so west of the Buntingford bypass along the A507 to Baldock, has nothing hidden – in fact, the rather remote church of St. James claims to be the highest, and therefore, most exposed in the county. And it is the church with the upper part of the tower in red brick with a top heavy look because of an octagonal stair turret corbel-led out below in an ogee form, which is the reason for our brief visit. This upper stage is dated 1660, plain to see picked out in an ornate brick panel, although the lower stage is of flint and 13th century.

No resident vicar and the key has to be obtained from Buntingford, but inside are a 15th century font, choir stalls with carvings of acrobats on the poppyhead ends and angels have been holding up the roof ever since the middle of the 17th century.

Tring

◄━ The most 'hidden' bit of Tring is dealt with under Wigginton because the interesting part of Tring Park, formerly the home of the Rothschild family, is cut off from the town by the A41(M).

The second Baron established the Tring Zoological Museum (now a branch of the Natural History section of the British Museum) in Akeman Street and just round the corner are the Louisa Cottages, estate cottages of 1893 and 1901.

The town is very ancient, near to the crossing of the Bronze Age Icknield Way and Roman Akeman Street, and shown in Domesday Book as Tredung or Tredunga, but it was only the building of the Grand Union Canal which brought it out of agricultural isolation. Today many new houses have expanded the town toward the reservoirs built between 1802 and 1839, but there is little to note apart from the church. Do not be misled by the look of the half-timbered Rose and Crown – it is all pseudo of circa 1905!

The church of St. Peter and St. Paul is embattled through-out with gargoyles below the parapet of the tower which was begun in the 14th century. Inside there are more curious figures on the corbels of the nave roof – a fox running off with a goose, a monkey with a book and a bottle, a chained bear et al. Much of the interior is new from the 1882 restoration but the 'sumptuous' Gore Monument of 1707 remains intact: the Gores owned Tring Park before the Rothschilds.

On your way to Long Marston or Puttenham, make a little diversion along Miswell Lane towards the Bucks boundary and you will see Goldfield Tower Mill which has been cleverly absorbed into a house with observation windows in the cap.

Wadesmill with Thundridge

➤ Wadesmill, on Roman Ermine Street, the old London Road to Royston and now the A10, was the place where the first turnpike gate was set up in 1663. Wadesmill is the name which travellers remember but, in reality, it is all part of Thundridge which has its own hidden bit of history in the tower, down by the river and covered in creeper, which is all that remains of the original Norman parish church. The bells of this old church were hung in the new St. Mary's church when it was built in 1853.

The new church has a stair turret higher than the top of the parapet which is not embattled and so is, as Pevsner says, 'alien to Herts' and it need not concern us further. Some inns, both in Thundridge and Wadesmill, have quite old histories reflecting busy coaching days which was the reason for the turnpike being set up – a toll was levied to help maintenance of the poor roads. But it is the bridge over the river Rib which should not be missed and is best seen from the garden of The Anchor.

This bridge, built in 1825, is unique in its construction and, as John Brushe wrote in *Hertfordshire Past*, 'Hertfordshire is not rich in bridges and of these Wadesmill is by far the most remarkable'. The bridge, composed of two arches of brick, rests uniquely on a colonnade of six Greek Doric columns of Cornish granite making it not merely decorative but structurally sound.

Walkern

━━ At Bassus Green, just to the east of the village, are the remains of some castle earthworks, although nearly obliterated by the farm buildings of Walkern Bury Farm. In St. Mary's church there is a Saxon stone rood so it can be seen that Walkern has a long history. Walchra in Domesday Book, the survey showed mills being operated by the river Beane but the most recent mill was built in 1828 and is now derelict.

Many farms in the parish have seen many centuries, some being actually in the village itself including 17th century

The octagonal dovecote at Walkern

151

Manor Farm with its octagonal dovecote right by the road-side. The birds have flown now and its cupola has been glazed in, but otherwise it will remain intact as a listed building.

The remains of the Saxon rood and the Saxon nave are the most ancient relics in the church but there is much work of the early Norman years. There is also a font of the late 14th century and the pulpit is early 16th century, but older than either of these is the remarkable marble figure of a knight lying in a recess clad from head to foot in chain mail. This mid 13th century effigy of a knight has the face hidden by the vizor of his flat-topped helmet, which is rare – there are only three such in all England.

In the churchyard there is a memorial to one Susannah Lewis who died in 1765 – it is, as Pevsner calls it, 'a scrolly obelisk on four scrolly feet'. Another lady of Walkern who will be remembered much more often, because she has gone into the history books, is Jane Wenham. She was the last person to be condemned to death for 'witchcraft' in England in 1711 but, due to the good offices of the Judge himself, she was granted the Queen's pardon and, too terrified to return to Walkern, was given a cottage at Hertingfordbury where she lived under the protection of Earl Cowper until she died in 1730. The case, undoubtedly, helped to pave the way for the Witchcraft Act of 1735 when the death penalty was abolished and 'witchhunting' ridiculed into oblivion.

Wallington

A remote village with a pond full of ducks which, like Ayot St. Lawrence, would not be on any itinerary except for the fact that, off and on over four years, George Orwell lived in the cottage called Monks Fitchett in Kit's Lane. His real name was Eric Blair, and it was as Eric Blair that he kept the village stores from about 1936 until 1940. The majority of the villagers would not have known any other name but he wrote *The Road to Wigan Pier* here: *1984* was to come later.

The grey flint-rubble St. Mary's church beside another pond is the other interest here, with many 15th century open benches still in use and well preserved. There is much 15th century detail – the tower, south porch and a screen with simple tracery – but a treasure is the original roof of the north aisle with angels at the base of each of the four main timber beams. These are comparatively rare in the county, although much more common in East Anglia, and were missed by Pevsner.

Waltham Cross

➤ Waltham Cross owes its name to the Cross which Edward I erected in 1294 in memory of his wife, Queen Eleanor and now a complete locality has taken its name from it, although technically it is part of Cheshunt (see Cheshunt), with no doubt the position of the Cross being a constant traffic hazard through the ages. Why is it there at all and not in Essex? A brief retelling of the story reveals all.

Queen Eleanor, the beloved wife of King Edward I, died in 1290 at Harby in Nottinghamshire while travelling to join her husband in the north of England. The grief stricken King accompanied the cortege back to London for her burial in Westminster Abbey, and each night her body was rested en route – in this locality it was at Waltham Abbey in Essex. The King later commanded that a memorial Cross should be built at each of the nightly resting places on the 13 day journey. As the Abbey was off the actual route, it was decided to build Waltham's Cross on the path of the actual route, open country at the end of the 13th century.

The previous night the Queen's body had been rested at St. Albans, but the Cross built there, very close to where the Clock Tower is now, was demolished in 1701. Only two other Eleanor Crosses survive and both of these are in Northamptonshire – that at Charing Cross is only a replica – so the greatest care must be taken to preserve this priceless antiquity.

The Eleanor Cross at Waltham Cross

The Cross, with a little restoration from time to time, has stood for over 700 years, and hopefully it will continue to do so for many more. Modern buildings and traffic now crowd around it, and you will look in vain for the Four Swans Inn – all that is left is a new sign over the road which was put up to replace the original sign after the inn was demolished when the Shopping Pavilion was built.

Nothing more need have been said about Waltham Cross if it was not for the fact that Anthony Trollope, the famous novelist had lived there from 1859 until 1871. He was an Inspector of Postal Services and is credited with being the genius behind the introduction of the pillar box. He was already a successful novelist when he moved into Waltham House in 1859 and stayed on for four years after his retirement from the Postal Service in 1867 and then putting his house on the market in 1871. Today, by an extraordinary coincidence the Waltham Cross Sorting Office stands on the site of his old house – a well deserved, albeit unsuspected, posthumous tribute to the originator of the pillar box!

Ware

To older generations Ware only meant 'The Great Bed of Ware' which for four centuries has been a source of amusement because of its size – nearly 11 feet square and over 7 feet high. It has often been mentioned in literature and Shakespeare has Sir Toby Belch making an amusing allusion to it in *Twelfth Night* when giving advice to Sir Andrew Aguecheek. After various vicissitudes and a spell of residence in Rye House (see Hoddesdon) it is hidden no longer because it has left Ware to become an exhibit in The Victoria and Albert Museum.

A most unusual feature, not often found in this country and certainly nowhere else in the county, is the sight of a number of gazebos, at the end of gardens leading down from the High Street, which look out over the river Lea. Very

155

many of them derelict for years, 1987 saw Civic Trust awards being made after their restoration.

Immediately after the gazebos, the river Lea flows past the grounds of the Priory Council Offices, a building which was bequeathed to the townsfolk after The First World War by Mrs. Anne Croft of the prosperous malting family when Ware was the centre of the malt trade in the county. The building still has 15th century remains of what was, before the Dissolution, a House of the Franciscan Order, and you do not have to visit the Council Offices to examine the exterior because it stands in public gardens.

Practically across the road is the spacious church of St. Mary, embattled all over and with its 5-stage tower overlooking the town. It is one of the oldest towers in the county dating from circa 1330 and the chancel dates from the 13th century but, as Pevsner says, 'It has been all too thoroughly restored'. Still, there are several interesting items including an octagonal font of circa 1380 which is of unusually fine workmanship being elaborately carved with figures of St. George and The Dragon, St. Christopher, the Virgin and Archangel Gabriel and others. Look out also for the late 17th century pulpit and there is a door of the 14th century from the chancel to the vestry which has three locks.

Down the High Street there are a number of old houses of the 16th and 17th centuries still surviving the developers, but many are hidden by later brick fronts. They reflect the period of the town's greatest prosperity when the old Market Place was still functioning. Facing what remains is the old Town Hall of 1827 which has been saved by enlightened planning and is now the offices of a firm of estate agents.

A few yards further east off East Street through an archway into Bluecoat Yard there is more hidden history. On the right is Place House, partly 14th century, which was the home of the original Bluecoat School before its removal to Hertford, and there are two plaques, one recording this fact and one after it was re-opened in 1978 after restoration, opposite a long terrace of almshouse-like cottages of 1698.

One more feature remains – John Scott's Grotto of circa

1760, now 'lost' in the middle of a modern housing estate opposite The College of Further Education. Unique in the county, it is open on the last Saturday in the months of April to September or by appointment through the Tourist Information Centre.

Waterford

◄ The old 1903 guidebook says of Waterford only that it is 'in Bengeo parish, on the river Beane. On the marsh is some grazing common, free to all parishioners'. Few parishioners today are likely to have anything to put out to graze. The County Council Highways Department occupies the neo-Tudor 'Goldings' of circa 1871-7 (at one time a Dr. Barnado Home) so we must turn to the little church which stands demurely by the gates, looking rather ordinary from the exterior.

Robert Abel-Smith, a wealthy banker, built the church at the same time that he built 'Goldings' and inside, instead of bits and pieces of an earlier church on the site because there was none, this church is filled with a fabulous collection of stained glass by the Pre-Raphaelite group William Morris and Co. Pevsner writes: 'an excellent display for studying the different qualities of the individual artists who worked for the firm'. William Morris, who depicted the Archangel Gabriel and the Virgin Mary, Philip Webb, Burne-Jones, Selwyn Image, Ford Madox Brown and even the great Dante Gabriel Rossetti himself, who was their stimulus – they are all here.

Watford

◄ A very good book entitled *History of Watford* by W. R. Saunders, originally published in 1931 but updated and republished in 1986, gives you all you need to know about the history of Watford and about some of the old buildings. To supplement that there is one of the best Town Guides that I have seen which is a mine of information on Watford – its industries, all the social amenities and, of course, the local football club!

Ted Parrish, in his foreword to the new edition of *History of Watford*, praises the work of W. R. Saunders but he adds: 'In his wildest dreams he could not have envisaged the destruction of a town which now exists only in obscure corners of our memories and in the corridors of time'. With that in mind, whatever can be left to be revealed? Rest assured, however – all is not lost!

St. Mary's church, lying just off the High Street and thus virtually in the centre of the town, is undoubtedly Watford's most ancient monument although no part of the existing building dates from earlier than 1230. Happily, in a town which boasts all kinds of tall buildings including massive stacking car parks, St. Mary's is not completely swamped because the flint tower, topped by its spike, rises to 100 feet. The church is entered through the Church Centre which was built between 1977 and 1979 and financed partly by the congregation 'without impairing normal giving!'. Great care was taken to ensure that the new building blended with the old.

In the north chancel is what is known as the Essex Chapel where the monuments by Nicholas Stone are some of the best in the county but get a copy of the church guide for full details. The font is comparatively modern having been installed during the extensive restoration of 1871 but fragments of a 12th century font were discovered then, were put together and now it is in use in St. James' church in Watford Fields. It is, according to *History of Watford*, the oldest piece of architecture in Watford.

Part of the sum needed for the Church Centre was obtained by selling the lease of Mrs. Elizabeth Fuller's Free School, the listed building of 1704 which faces the Centre across the churchyard. Only a few yards away are the Bedford Almshouses in George Street which were founded in 1580. Founded by the 8th Earl of Bedford, they were saved from demolition in 1931 and now, after considerable modernisation, this provision for 'eight poor women' is the oldest inhabited group of buildings in the town.

As a sign of the times in our changing society, do not miss the neat little Jamia Mosque situated quietly on the edge of the Ring Road whilst just south of the Ring Road, on Lower High Street, is the Watford Museum, formerly the offices of Benskins the brewers, which opened in 1981. Benskins had, by using the building as offices, already saved one of Watford's treasures, a typically solid 18th century Georgian dwelling house.

A building, virtually hidden, of a century earlier, is the former Dower House (of the now demolished Cassiobury mansion) which still stands right by the Technical College and is now the District Education Office. Completely overshadowed by the College and with no mention in the guidebook, it is, nevertheless, what Pevsner calls 'the best classical house in Watford'.

Cassiobury House, the former seat of the Earls of Essex, was demolished in 1927 but leaving a park for public use through which flows the river Gade and the Grand Union Canal. If you follow the canal north for about a mile you come to the Grove Mill (converted into flats in 1974) and then an elegant balustraded bridge of circa 1800 which was refurbished in 1987 to celebrate 190 years of this stretch of the canal. The track over the bridge leads on to The Grove, the former home of the Earl of Clarendon, now in use as a Training Centre for British Transport.

Watton-at-Stone

This large village, now blessed with a bypass, owes its name to a milestone said to have stood alongside the Waggon and Horses at the north end of the village. Popular belief, on the other hand, according to the WI Book says that the village acquired the suffix '-at-Stone' because of two large rocks of Hertfordshire puddingstone. You takes your choice!

The best thing in the village, according to Pevsner, is a baluster-shaped early 19th century cast-iron pump which had an oak cover put over it with an inscription in memory of Lt. Gen. Philip Smith CB Grenadier Guards who died in 1894. Some, locally, may think otherwise because, quite against the trend, the village recently managed to have the station re-opened after many years of closure: that, for many, must have been the 'best thing' for years!

In the now quieter High Street, there are a number of cottages more than 300 years old including the George and Dragon first licenced 1603 and, close to the pump, Watton Hall which is mainly late 16th century but has earlier trefoil brick arches.

In the parish church of St. Andrew and St. Mary, there are memorials to a variety of past noblemen including a number of former residents of the earlier mansion on the Woodhall Park site, from as early as 1361. The present building of 1771 is now a preparatory school. The church is an all-embattled flint one, rebuilt so completely in the 15th century that all trace of any earlier history was destroyed. However, it is not without interest because not only has it a stair turret rising higher than the tower battlements but it has two porches, the north porch having two storeys with a stair turret of its own.

Welwyn

Inevitably this large village will be lumped together with big-brother Garden City but, perhaps because of the A1(M), it has been saved from being absorbed. The Little Guide, written before any idea of a Garden Suburb was mooted, calls it 'a small town which can show little of interest beyond many quaint cottages and the church'. Today, although independent, it is largely a commuter sub-urb, with the larger neighbour having the shopping centre and the supermarkets.

A number of large houses of the 18th or 19th centuries, once in private hands, remain but The Frythe is ICI, Danesbury is a hospital and Lockleys, on the other side of the motorway, is part of Sherrardswood School. In the grounds of Lockleys, a Roman villa of the 1st century A.D. was excavated whilst recently a Roman Baths was found, and is preserved in a special vault actually under the motorway, although open to the public at certain times.

Up till 1927, the main road went through the village so, like some other places, there are remains of coaching inns here, particularly the Wellington, formerly called The Swan and mentioned by Pepys in 1664, and the 17th century or earlier White Hart. The Wellington is diagonally opposite the church of St. Mary but right on the edge of the churchyard is a much restored half-timbered house of circa 1450 which has served a number of purposes in its time: church hall, almshouse, workhouse and labelled 'poor house' in the 1910 Royal Commission Inventory but 'now the police station'. (R. Lydekker has a photograph of it in his 1909 book on the county with the same caption!) Branch Johnson left a note to say that 'it became the police station about 1868, remaining so until about the period of World War I. Later it became the post office'.

St. Mary's has no great architectural feature of note, especially after rebuilding by Blomfield of the south chancel chapel in 1911. There are, however, Roman bricks in the church walls and some grotesque corbels of the 13th century in the south aisle. Perhaps to some people the most important item is the mural tablet to Dr. Edward Young, rector here from 1730 to 1765 and buried in the church. He wrote the once celebrated *The Complaint or Night Thoughts on Life, Death and Immortality* in which is the immortal phrase, 'procrastination is the thief of time!'

Welwyn Garden City

Planned as a town after the First World War and, under the guidance of Ebenezer Howard, the founders learned from the mistakes of the earlier pioneers at Letchworth. The situation changed in 1948 when it was designated as one of the post-war New Towns under a Development Corporation also responsible for Hatfield New Town. There was a proviso to this that there should be country left between them: it can be said that this has been achieved by the fine boating and sailing lakes in Stanborough Park through which the river Lea flows.

The industrial area was kept to the east of the main railway line to Edinburgh with the Shredded Wheat Factory, designed by the chief architect of Welwyn Garden City, Louis de Soissons, in 1925 having become famous all over the world typifying 'the Modern Factory' of the post-First World War years. It is, however, The Parkway on the civic side with the de Soissons Memorial at the north end which gives the place an almost continental aspect which is helped considerably by the Coronation Fountain.

If the de Soissons Memorial, which was unveiled by HM Queen Elizabeth, The Queen Mother in 1970, is so very open for all to see and use in its setting inside the semi-circular Campus, Ebenezer Howard's is the very opposite and virtually hidden unless you are alert. It is a bronze plaque flat on the ground and set in cobbles in the Howardsgate Gardens, roughly between the Post Office and W. H. Smith's shop. It replaces a wall memorial which used to be at the top of Parkway but surely he deserves better: still, he was a modest man and perhaps he would have been the last to complain!

South of the Fountain is something a little more conspicuous – a sculptured stone figure called *Dawn* by David Evans who died in 1959 is situated between the two carriageways of The Parkway.

The story of Welwyn Garden City has been well

documented and many books are available so read all about it. Maybe, however, the oldest buildings are not mentioned because they are hidden away off the main road. The oldest farm cottage, of what in the 13th century was a separate place called Haneshyde, is dated 1604 and still stands in Bridge Road, whilst in Handside Road is Handside Farmhouse which is a Grade II listed buildling.

West Hyde

West Hyde earns its place because it is the most southerly village in the county, and although not, apparently, meriting a place in Domesday Book, there are mentions as long ago as 796 A.D. The A412 between Rickmansworth and Denham, or, to be more practical, between Watford and Slough which was constantly choked at Maple Cross, has now been relieved by the opening of the M25, and West Hyde is quiet once more – almost water-logged with lakes, the river Colne and the Grand Union Canal.

The West Hyde Lock is picturesque when viewed from the road bridge, but only pleasure craft are seen now on the canal. There are one or two old private houses, like half-timbered Corner Hall, still surviving despite the encroachment of gravel pits and there is little St. Thomas' church, only built in 1844, which the Little Guide calls 'Italian in style'.

Westmill

The quintessence of the English Village – more compact than Benington and, because of its size, looking very neat and perhaps a trifle smug. Nevertheless, just the place to take the Overseas Visitor who wants to see the 'Ideal English Village'!

The little village green with its old roofed pump looks down on a cluster of picturesque cottages and houses with the spiked tower of St. Mary's church to be seen behind the television aerials which unfortunately, as elsewhere, do detract a little from the 'olde worlde' look. Enjoy the visual attraction of Westmill and note Westmill Bury, the manor house with its huge barn but, a short distance away from the village, is a curiosity which, fortunately, has survived. Between Cherry Green and the earthworks of the deserted village of Wakeley is Button Snap, the only property ever owned by Charles Lamb. In one of the *Essays of Elia* he writes somewhat mockingly: 'When I journeyed down to take possession, and planted foot on my own ground . . . I strode with the feeling of an English freeholder that all betwixt sky and centre was my own'. That was in 1812 but he never lived in it and he sold it for £50!

Back in the village near The Sword in Hand and through the lychgate, St. Mary's has an ancient history with pre-Conquest nave although it was much restored, over-restored as one authority has it, in 1875. On the other hand, it has exciting points of interest including the rare stone angels with flaming torches guarding the west door from well before the Reformation. Below the pargetting of the spiked and embattled tower, which is normal for the county, are gargoyles but in the tower itself, among the five bells is one of circa 1350 inscribed 'William Rofforde made me'. Unfortunately, the bells cannot be rung, as the little church guide-book tells us, unless extensive structural work is undertaken.

Before you leave the church, take a look at the choir stalls with their poppyheads and unusually long carved gaunt-looking human heads on either side of the chancel – these are all 16th century.

Weston

A long straggling village with Holy Trinity church on the eastern edge up a lane which ends in a car park. By a coincidence, a derelict tower mill, minus cap, stands almost equidistant on the western edge.

The church was restored in the 19th century but the north transept, nave and the lower part of the tower are all of an early 12th century cruciform building. The upper part of the tower only dates from 1867, note the little turret and a particularly large weathervane cockerel. Another 15th century font here and note that the nave ceiling is divided into panels with the roof beams resting on grotesque stone heads. It is in the churchyard, however, that perhaps there is the most interesting fact to remember about Weston. The grave of 'Jack O'Legs', a local 'giant' and, indeed, a local 'Robin Hood' who robbed the rich to feed the poor, is reputedly buried between the two stones that are just by the church gate.

The story goes that, after being caught and condemned to death, Jack made one last request, that he might be buried where his arrow struck the ground. The arrow flew through the air, glanced off the roof of the church and fell between the two stones 14 feet apart. A similar tale is told about Robin Hood's valiant henchman, Little John, in Derbyshire but it makes a lovely legend.

The village has a number of road crossings in it which help to make spaces for little greens and a pond. A mixture of half-timbered and modern houses do their best to conceal a small factory here, the place where Guardsmen's busbies are made.

Wheathampstead

Is it the sound of the clash of Roman swords against the primitive weapons of the Catuvellauni fighting under their chieftain Cassivellaunus, or is it just the busy combine in the field close by harvesting the wheat which may have helped to form the name of this very ancient village? Find out by going along the Marford Road and then up the little lane opposite The Nelson with a signpost pointing to 'Devil's Dyke' – there are the real remains of one of the earliest battles ever fought on British soil.

Now under the protection of the National Trust there are 78 acres of agricultural land which was the oppidum or 'town redoubt', flanked on two sides by the ramparts, The Slad and The Devil's Dyke (both clearly marked on the OS map), where the combined forces of several tribes of the Belgae, under the elected leader Cassivellaunus, were defeated by the Romans under Julius Caesar on his second foray into Britain in 54 B.C. Not, perhaps, very exiciting to look at now but let your imagination run riot – the evidence is definitely still there after 2000 years.

Some scholars believe that the village name derives from the 'wetness' of the marshland surrounding it in those ancient times. Be that as it may, the river Lea flows under the road and the ancient mill of the 16th century at the bottom of the High Street.

Across the road but on opposite banks of the river, stands the 16th century Wheathampstead Place, one-time offices of Murphy Chemicals, and the 17th century Bull Inn. The railway link between Hatfield and Luton disappeared when Dr. Beeching wielded the axe, and now the former Railway Hotel has been renamed The Abbot John. He was born in the parish, became a Benedictine monk and was the 33rd Abbot of St. Albans Abbey for 30 years until his death in 1465, a wise, good and liberal man.

Another public house which cannot be overlooked stands on the edge of Nomansland, and was renamed The Wicked Lady after the exploits of Lady Katherine Ferrers and the scene of her mortal wounding (see Markyate).

The parents of Abbot John, Hugo and Margaret Bostock, are remembered on a brass in St. Helen's church, mainly of the 13th century but there is evidence of an earlier Saxon church – certainly Wheathampstead has its place in Domesday Book with a church as part of the inventory. St. Helen's, the only church dedicated to this saint in the county, has an unusual broach spire with strips of lead arranged in a herringbone pattern looking like a huge inverted ice-cream cone! There are many interesting features inside so refer to the church history and guide for full details, but do not miss the statue in the north transept of Apsley Cherry-Garrard who was in Captain Scott's expedition to the South Pole in 1910, and was with the search party that discovered the bodies of Scott and his companions. He later wrote *The Worst Journey in the World*, which has become a minor classic, telling the whole story.

Whitwell

➤ Whitwell has no church – it is essentially a hamlet in the parish of St. Paul's Walden – but it has the larger population.

A walk up and down the High Street is rewarded by Georgian houses with here and there some half-timbering, particularly on the corner leading down to the river Mimram opposite the Eagle and Child. This old inn has a date 1747 but is obviously much older.

A little way along towards the St. Paul's Walden turning is the half-timbered Bull and The Old Brewery, now a dwelling, but do not miss the 17th century village hall with its dormer windows.

Widford

➤ More Charles Lamb associations here (see Harpenden and Westmill) and a place of pilgrimage for all lovers of his works. His grandmother, Mary Field, who was housekeeper at Blakesware for over half a century, lies buried in the little churchyard of St. John The Baptist's church which stands on the western edge of the village. Note that the stonemason carved 'Feild' on her gravestone in error.

Charles Lamb and his sister Mary often used to stay with

their grandmother until she died in 1792, and he grew to love Blakesware. It was demolished in 1823 and this distressed him very much – a distress which is expressed fully in one of his *Essays of Elia*, 'Blakesmoor in H......Shire'. A new house was built between 1876–9 in neo-Tudor style, and the OS map shows it as 'Monastery'.

In the village are a number of attractive houses, all privately owned of course, and on the wall of The Bell Inn is a plaque commemorating Charles Lamb and the fact that he 'frequented this Inn for many years'.

The one house which is worthy of our attention is 17th century Widfordbury, now a farmhouse, but it shares with the church next door a wall of an earlier period probably early 16th century, and said locally to have belonged to a former priory. There is a most interesting gateway with an arch, and a moulded plinth runs along the wall on the churchyard side, whilst on the farm side is an octagonal dovecote.

The church is unusual because it has two lychgates – one, to the church itself, was built to commemorate the Diamond Jubilee of Queen Victoria whilst the other was put up as a war memorial to those who fell in both wars and acts as an entrance to a second churchyard across the road.

The oldest part of the church, built in the 13th century or earlier, was considerably extended in the 14th century, and it is of this date that the chief treasure belongs – the five wall paintings which were restored in 1936 by Professor Tristram. Tall figures on either side of the east window, a bishop on the right and possibly The Annunciation on the left, but the finest is on the north wall depicting the patron saint of the church with the flashing sword indicative of his martyrdom.

There is a north doorway of circa 1370 with even earlier ironwork, an octagonal font carved with heads of a lion and a nun dating from circa 1420 and more paintings on the ceiling of the chancel which were completed and dedicated in 1883. On leaving the church, after noting the Norman zigzag above the south door, you can hardly miss the copper spire of 1888 on top of the 14th century tower.

Wigginton

➤ Forget Tring, drive under the east end of the all-too-short A41(M) and immediately there is a decision to make – right or left fork? Whichever road you take, the end product is Wigginton from where, on a spur of the Chilterns, you obtain glorious views across to Ashridge and the Bridgewater Monument rising above Aldbury, eastwards back to Berkhamsted, westwards towards Aylesbury and southwards over the Champneys 'Health Farm' towards Chesham.

The little church of St. Bartholomew was virtually rebuilt in 1881, although basically a late medieval one and there is still what is known as the West Chamber (the Weedon Chapel) dating from the 15th century forming an extension to the nave.

Between Wigginton and Champneys is Grim's Ditch, an earthwork of Saxon or even Iron Age origin, no-one is quite sure, but it is in the opposite direction in the woods of Tring Park that unexpected surprises await those who care to search.

At the turn of the century many of the villagers worked for, and lived in houses owned by, Lord Rothschild of Tring Park but now that the A41(M) has cut the park in two the woods virtually 'belong' to Wigginton. An opening at the end of a cul-de-sac of houses just at the crest of that right fork leads into the woods and there you will find the ruinous 18th century summer house in the form of a Greek temple with a four column Ionic portica. It is almost complete, however, less so than the other surprise – a tall obelisk to the memory of Nell Gwynne who used to stay at the original Tring Park manor house with Charles II.

Willian

➤ My Little Guide of 1903 has this to say about it: 'Willian, formerly Wylie, is very ancient', and, in fact, it is in Domesday Book as Wilie. Now part of Letchworth, but it still retains the look of a village having been saved so far from being engulfed because of its position. There is much of interest within a small area but take great care despite a supposed speed limit through the village – it is on a 'rat run' from the A1(M) to the Letchworth Hall Hotel and to part of the Garden City!

Noticeable at once, when approaching from the A1(M), are groups of cottages with names and dates on them – Roxley, Manor and Lordship dated either 1868 or 1870 – and then, in pristine condition, a timber-framed thatched cottage called 'The Old Vicarage' standing right by the lychgate leading into the church of All Saints. It is not known when this was last a vicarage, and the lychgate is a war memorial to those who fell in the Second World War but the church has some most unusual features. A simple building of nave and chancel of the 12th century, with the tower added circa 1430, a new pitched roof was built to replace a faulty flat roof in 1870 when, as can be seen, much rebuilding was taking place all over the village.

The old guidebooks *and* Pevsner tell of chancel stalls with poppyheads and strange carvings. These have now been removed and the altar brought forward in very recent years, but three of the poppyheads with the strange carvings have been made into a seat. The back has an elephant complete with a howdah, whilst one side has a sphinx-like monster with a barbed tail above John the Baptist's head on a charger. The screen has gone as well but on both sides of the chancel are the remains of what appears to be filled-in sedilia with a number of heads looking in three directions at once.

The west door in the base of the tower has shields above it, and very worn human faces on either side but to me the chief glory here is the clutch of gargoyles around the outside of the parapet of the tower – arguably the finest in the county, yet unsung and unrecorded, even in the church guide. Arthur Mee has the only record I have found and he writes of 'gargoyles of death and the other dread powers peering out from the 15th century tower'. (See Great Gaddesden).

Still in the village, note the 7-bay Punchardon Hall, originally of the 17th century but refaced with brick in the 18th century, which stands opposite The Fox Inn, and a large village pond on the same side as Punchardon Hall. Then, a mile or so along the narrow road to Great Wymondley, there is a roadside memorial to two 'aviators' of the Royal Flying Corps who were killed in a flying accident on 6th September 1912 – the very first airmen to be killed, as the memorial says, 'whilst serving their Country'.

Wilstone

➤ Bounded on the north by the Grand Union Canal and the south by reservoirs, Wilstone is so often ignored in the guidebooks – not a word in Pevsner or Arthur Mee, although it does get a mention in my trusty Little Guide of 1903. It does, however, complete a triangle of villages in the odd spit of land projecting north-west of Tring. It shows no particular trait that marks it out as part of Hertfordshire, and the little flint church of 1860 has no tower, embattled or otherwise, because, although one was in the plans, the money ran out.

A little village green overlooked by half-timbered Paddock Cottage is a focal point whilst the Half Moon Inn cannot be overlooked, but one other important point must be mentioned. Long Marston is the village usually connected with the last 'witch' tragedy but some authorities claim that the pond in which the unfortunate couple were drowned was in Wilstone!

Wormley

━► Trapped between Cheshunt and Broxbourne, it was originally to be part of the Broxbourne entry but a place with an entry in Domesday Book as Wermelae certainly deserves better.

The New river runs parallel with the old main road, and now that the A10 trunk road has taken through traffic, it is easier to see that a few 17th and 18th century houses still survive in the rather dreary road which runs along the eastern flank of the county.

Across the A10 is Wormleybury, built between 1767 and 1769 by Robert Mylne, at the time also architect to the New River Company (see Great Amwell). In 1782 he added a giant portico on the entrance side but Robert Adam was responsible for embellishment inside. Not open to the public as a stately home, apartments are rented out by the present owners who live in the stable block with its fine clock turret. To the west of the house is an ornamental lake, really a widening of a stream, with an eye-catcher of a big urn on the other side. It is dedicated to a racehorse, so successful that the winnings paid for the building of the mansion!

Further on is the church of St. Laurence, surely one of the oldest in the county but with no tower, only a bellcote of 1826. The nave was built at the beginning of the 12th century and the north doorway and a window in the north wall are of the same century whilst there is a 13th century doorway in the south aisle. The chancel has been much restored and so has lost any original features but there is a 'Last Supper' painting from Italy as a reredos, presented by the then owner of Wormleybury, Sir Abraham Hume, in 1797. There is also a magnificent alabaster wall monument to William Purveye and his family: William Purveye was Steward to Sir Robert Cecil and died in 1617. There is also a font of an unusual design, again of the 12th century, and a Jacobean pulpit.

Wyddial

➤ The little scattered hamlet of Wyddial, which lies on a link road between the A10 north of Buntingford and the B1368 leading to Barley and Barkway, has an entry in Domesday Book as Widihale and was given by the Conqueror to Hardwin de Scalers. My little 1903 guidebook says 'the walk from Buntingford up the hill to the ruined church of Layston (see Buntingford) and thence to this village, leads through some of the quietest spots in the county' – nothing much seems to have changed and there does not appear to have been much development since 1086!

It has, nevertheless, several houses of character including Wyddial Hall just north of the church and a half-timbered farmhouse, with its additional modern buildings, on the other side of the road to the church. It is the church of St. Giles, one of only three dedicated to that saint in the county, which is the chief reason for a visit but, unfortunately, it probably remains locked for most of the time. Locked or not, a visit will be rewarded by seeing that the whole of the north side is completely built of brick dated 1532 and, as Pevsner writes, 'this triumphant entry of brick into church building is a significant sign of the Tudor age'.

There used to be, until very recently, several box pews still remaining in this church but I understand that they had to be dismantled due to damp. I certainly could not see them in my attempts to look into the church through the one unstained clear glass window!

Index